The Entrepreneur's Guide to

Sleaze-Free Selling

The 3-Step Sales Formula for Growing Your Business ... Without Being Obnoxious, Pushy or Rude

Julia Kline

www.SleazeFreeSelling.com

Copyright 2013 by Julia Kline

Table of Contents

Preface: How This Book Got Its Heart 5

About the Author 8

Introduction: Is This Book For You? 10

Disclaimers 14

Part 1: Laying the Foundation

Chapter 1: The Trap of the Sleazy Salesperson 12

Chapter 2: One Simple Step to De-Sleaze Your Entire Sales Process 23

Chapter 3: How to Avoid Customers That Bring Out the Sleaze In You 37

Chapter 4: Turning "No" Into "Yes" ... The Non-Sleazy Way 59

Part 2: Turning the Sleaze-Free Sales Formula into Cash

Chapter 5: How to Get All the Customers You'll Ever Need 75

Chapter 6: How to talk to a potential customer about buying, without feeling like a sleaze-ball 125

Chapter 7: Never again allow even a single sale to slip through your fingers 144

Conclusion and Next Steps 165

Appendix A: Follow-up Email Sequence 169

Preface: How This Book Got Its Heart

As a business owner, you know there is no more powerful tool in your arsenal than the ability to effectively sell your products and services. Sales is the lifeblood of your business.

With lots of sales coming in the door, your shop buzzes. (Whether your "shop" is a physical store, an online entity, or just you at your desk with a telephone). Your employees are all busy, the bills are all paid, the checks you take home each month make you do a happy dance - all the way to the bank.

Without sales coming in however, it's a very different story. The bell on the front door never rings, the cash register sits empty, dust gathers on your shelves. And your self-esteem, self-confidence, and general sense of well-being? Those all slowly disintegrate, to be replaced by self-doubt, disappointment and dejection - maybe even anxiety, depression and hopelessness.

I know. I've been there. After becoming a millionaire for the first time before the age of 30, I crashed into a wall in my early 30's. Market forces had changed, and the industry that had made me wealthy was no longer viable for me. So I switched gears and started another business - one that should have been lucrative. But instead, my business floundered for five long years, while I dragged along somewhere close to bottom, experiencing frequent bouts of severe depression.

While I wouldn't have admitted it to myself at the time, the reason my business floundered so long is because I wasn't selling enough. I wasn't getting out there, telling people about what I did, and asking them to pay me for it.

What I learned during those five dark years of "doing it wrong" is the heart of this book.

Notice what I said - the lessons from my dark years are the _heart_ of this book. I did not say those lessons make up the _content_ of this book. This book's content is drawn from my successes - the tactics I've learned and then implemented, throughout my career, to successfully grow business after business for myself and my clients.

But my dark years are when I learned about my own heart - my weaknesses, and ultimately, my strengths. I experienced disappointment and self-loathing, as one feeble attempt after another met with "failure." I wrestled with depression, as the greatness I knew I had inside me lay dormant, and nothing I did seemed able to bring it out. I finally found the courage to face my real fears - the biggees - when absolutely nothing else had worked, and I was flat-out desperate for a change.

Does any of this sound familiar? If so, keep reading. You're in the right place.

Only by agonizing with those wrenching emotions was I finally able to get in touch with my heart. And by touching my own heart, I also learned how to touch my customers' hearts. Much to my surprise, it turned out that being REAL, and being HUMAN, is a much faster and sturdier path to both personal power and financial success than any slippery, sleazy sales tactics I had ever learned or used before.

That's why I say that this transformation of mine - the plunge into darkness, and the long haul to get back out again - is the heart of this book. It infuses every chapter, every page, every tactic and strategy I'll be teaching you.

So this is no ordinary sales book. Rather, it is a manual for significant success in your business and your life. Success that results from sales, but which is only made possible by opening your heart.

I'd like to thank the following people for helping to make this book possible:

Jo Anne Cunnington, my Sales Director at Mary Kay, and Ted Sveda, my Sales Manager when I was in real estate. From them, I learned how to sell snow to an eskimo.

Leonie Gully and Marilyn Delucca - messengers who showed up at just the right time along my journey, to help me crack open my heart.

Baeth Davis, my friend and guide, for shining a soft gentle light on my true path.

Most of all my father, for his absolutely unwavering support of me. Throughout even my darkest years, when everyone else told you to give up on me, you believed in me, Dad. I wouldn't have made it without you. Thank you. I love you.

About the Author

Julia Kline has had a diverse career - everything from Chicago Public Schoolteacher to Mary Kay lady to real estate developer to platform speaker to marketing consultant.

But all the businesses Julia's been in required one thing - *excellent salesmanship.*

Julia mastered the technical aspects of marketing and sales early in her career and could effortlessly sell snow to an eskimo. But then she had an aha moment that shifted how she viewed sales forever: eskimos don't need snow!

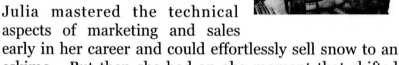

Ever since that revelation, Julia has focused on serving her customers, even as she was leading them through the sales process. She honors the trust that her customers and clients put in her, and strives to always provide solutions that are in their highest and best interests. While still, of course, maintaining an impressive sales record!

In her most recent book, "The Entrepreneur's Guide to Sleaze-Free Selling," Julia presents her unique blend of precision salesmanship and customer-focused authenticity in a sequence of steps that are easy to model.

~~~~~~~~~~~~~~~~~~~~~~~~~~~~~~~~~

Julia brings heart-centered salesmanship to the masses through her many books, courses, monthly publications and live events. She also does private consulting with a small handful of clients.

To learn more - and to sign up for Julia's sales & marketing newsletter - please visit:

http:// SleazeFreeSelling.com

Introduction: Is This Book For You?

This book is for you if:

It's very important to you to always be authentic and real with your customers

AND

You are eager to sell lots & lots of your products and services.

If you don't currently do an awesome job of selling and marketing your own business, go easy on yourself! This book is going to help you by leaps and bounds; but the first thing you need to do is quit beating yourself up for whatever you're doing (or not doing) now.

The aim of this book is to help you make a profound shift in the way you approach your customers. And by so shifting, begin to sell a lot more of your products and services.

If your approach, up until now, has frankly been kind of sleazy - then I hope what you learn in these pages will enlighten you. You'll see that not only will you feel better about yourself when you approach your customers as real people, rather than "targets," but you'll also sell more. The world is changing at a rapid pace; and the same old hard-sell tactics that may have worked once ... just don't anymore. (You probably already know that - and that's why you're reading this book in the first place).

It's more likely, however, that you're reading this book because you _hate_ the idea of being sleazy; and you believe, deep down, that sales is inherently sleazy. Therefore you don't sell very much at all.

But you also recognize that by not selling your products and services, you can't stay in business very long. So you're hoping - praying, even - that this book might somehow provide you a way out of this trap you feel caught in.

I promise you that it will. You _will_ learn how to sell your products and services more than you ever have before, so that your business can grow and thrive. And the formula I provide between the pages of this book will be not just palatable to you, it will completely transform how you view the process of going out in the world and offering your products and services for sale.

All you need to do is make a commitment. A commitment to not only reading this book, but also to completing the Action Plans at the end of every chapter.

When you complete all of this book's Action Plans:

- You'll no longer think of sales as the most distasteful part of your job as a business owner
- You'll be fired up to go out and sell a ton of your products and services
- You'll feel no hesitation or queasiness about telling customers how much you charge, and asking them to pay it
- You'll be eager to go out and meet lots of prospective new customers
- Your customers will feel equally eager to be having those conversations with you
- Best of all, you'll start making a whole lot more sales!

This book is divided into 2 parts:

The reason you're going to sell a lot more after reading this book is that it's not simply a sales manual. It's also a step by step blueprint for incorporating the fundamentals of the Sleaze-Free Sales Formula into every aspect of your business' sales and marketing process.

In Part 1, Laying the Foundation, I cover Marketing and Sales 101 - traditional topics like "Who's Your Ideal Customer" and "Overcoming Customer Objections." The twist is, I approach these topics from a Sleaze-Free mentality. Yes, it is possible to sell your products and services - and sell a lot of them - without being the slightest bit sleazy.

All it takes is completely over-turning everything you've ever thought was true about sales and marketing!

I guarantee this is _not_ the same-old, rehashed advice you've heard in every other sales book you've ever read. After you learn my Sleaze-Free Sales Formula, neither you nor your customers will ever again hide from selling conversations. Selling conversations - whether over the phone, in person, or online - will be educational and inspiring for your customers, and be both easy and successful for you.

So while you may think you know everything about marketing, do not skip over Part I. You'll be pleasantly surprised - even if you consider yourself a bit of a marketing genius - at how many times you'll find yourself pausing in thoughtful contemplation, as you ponder your own sales process and compare it to the sales process I lay out for you in Part 1 of this book.

Truly. Part I of this book can change not only your business, but also your life.

In Part 2, Turning the Sleaze-Free Sales Formula into Cash, I give you a blueprint for how to kick your marketing and sales up a notch. Because now that you'll have a marketing and sales process you can feel good about, you'll want to implement it a whole lot more.

So this is the section where we get tactical:
- How to find a whole lot more customers to talk to
- How to approach customers in a way that feels natural and easy - not sleazy or pitchy
- How to turn initial conversations into conversations about buying
- How to set yourself up for "yes" instead of "no" a lot more often
- How to stay in touch with the "no's" naturally and authentically - so you never again have to feel like you're bothering them when you send an email or make a phone call in order to turn them into a "yes."

Selling Online vs. Selling In Person

You might be wondering whether this book is about one-on-one, "belly to belly" sales, or if it's a book about how to attract customers with "mass marketing" methods like the internet, direct mail and broadcast advertising.

And actually, t's both.

When we're discussing how to be authentic with your customers, and how to come from a place that's heart-centered rather than sleazy, it's most useful to focus on one-on-one conversations with real people.

But once you get the hang of how to create authentic, heart-centered sales messages, you can use that same knowledge to turbo-charge your sales and marketing efforts everywhere: online, in print, with direct mail, or even over the broadcast airwaves.

The pages of this book guide you through both.

Disclaimers
(Legal and Otherwise)

I'm Julia Kline and I wrote the book you're about to read - every last word of it. I'm a salesperson, an intuitive, a coach, speaker, publisher, consultant and student of Life.

I am NOT:

- a lawyer. I don't think there's any legal advice in this book - but if there is, don't take it! Hire a lawyer!

- a CPA, bookkeeper or accountant. I don't think there's any financial advice in this book either - but if there is, don't take it! Hire a professional!

- a comedian. I think I'm pretty funny - but you might not. If you hate my jokes, just remind yourself it's not how I make my living.

- a technical wiz. I'm pretty good at turning a phrase, and sharing ideas that will make you think. What I have to say here might even improve both your life and your bottom line. But if you find typos, funky formatting or otherwise unacceptable written communication in this book - please spare me the negative reviews on those grounds alone.

(Emails to Feedback@SleazeFreeSelling.com will always be read however).

Lastly, nothing I've said in this book is a guarantee of success. I've made a lot of money in my career, and my clients have made a lot of money taking the advice I've given them. But that says nothing about whether YOU will succeed - especially if all you do is read this book. Success takes hard work. Lots of it.

That's why I've included an Action Plan at the end of each chapter. When you complete these Action Plans, your chances of success will be *much greater* (although still not guaranteed).

URGENT PLEA!!

Thank you for downloading my book. Please REVIEW this book on Amazon. I need your feedback to make the next version better.
(If Zoe can write a review, you can too!)

Thank you so much!

Part 1: Laying the Foundation

Chapter 1: The Trap of the Sleazy Salesperson

Given how important sales are to the success of your business, how come so many business owners shrink away from becoming master salespeople?

I'll tell you why: selling sucks!!

SELLING
SUCKS!!

Salespeople (and this includes you, if you're the owner of a small business) expose themselves to rejection on a daily basis, in big ways and small:

- dialing 100's of phone numbers that result in only voice messages
- reaching the end of a conversation with a potential customer and hearing the dreaded words, "I'll think about it"
- spending weeks nurturing a potential client through the sales process, only to have them buy from someone else

Each one of these scenarios leaves a pit in your stomach just thinking about it, doesn't it? It's no wonder that you as the business owner dread your role as a salesperson, and that you avoid it as much as possible. And becoming a master salesperson? Forget about it. Investing that kind of time in something you hate so much makes you want to poke your eye out with a stick!

Besides, salespeople are sleazy, right? Especially the good ones. And you certainly don't want to become one of _them_.

Good salespeople don't mean to be sleazy. (And by the way, _great_ salespeople aren't the slightest bit sleazy. That's what makes them great. More on that later in this book.)

Good salespeople have just built up such defenses against the constant barrage of rejection, that they've sort of lost touch with what it means to be human. They've forgotten that the person across the table from them - their potential customer - is a real person.

> This real person - the customer - has fears and insecurities about the buying process. They need a salesperson they can trust, not one who will manipulate their weaknesses.

> This real person - the customer - is savvy about the marketplace. They know what's a good deal and what's a rip-off. But they still need a knowledgeable salesperson to guide them to their best decision, not one who will constantly shove the salesperson's own products and services down their throat.

> This real person - the customer - has a problem they need solved. They _want_ to buy something! So they don't need to be "sold" so much as they need to be shown the way.

Being a salesperson who supports and serves the customer in these ways - in other words, one who isn't sleazy - isn't always easy. It requires you to go against a lot of your own human nature - to say nothing of conquer your own fears, insecurities and ego.

The world is filled with great books that answer the question of why customers don't buy, and that offer advice about how you can get them to buy.

But those books tend to be long and complicated - plus, of course, the advice they give you is the exact stuff that leaves you feeling like you need to take a shower!

The ironic thing is, the simpler you make the sales process, the more authentic and less sleazy it becomes as well.

If a customer isn't buying from you - they've said no to your pitch, or they haven't even stopped what they're doing long enough to hear your pitch in the first place - it's because they believe one of the following three things:

1. They think they don't have a problem
2. They doubt that you are somebody who can solve the problem
3. They're afraid it's going to be hard (or expensive, or time-consuming, or a hassle) to take the next step and buy something from you, in order to solve their problem.

That's it. There are no other reasons. If your customer didn't believe at least one of these things, they would buy from you. So your only job as a salesperson or business owner is naturally to overturn those three beliefs.

In other words, you need your prospective customer to now believe:

1. They have a Big Problem. Not only that, but it's getting bigger every day and they can't continue to live with this problem.
2. That you are the #1 best person to solve this Big Problem for them.
3. That taking the next step with you (buying something) is simple, painless and easy.

That's it! Getting your customer to believe those 3 little things is how you make a sale. Over and over and over again.

Really, that's it? Yes, really. That's it.

"But what about ability to pay?" you might ask. "I've often had customers who would love to buy from me - they believed all three of the things you just listed - but they simply couldn't afford it."

If you think customers don't buy from you because they can't afford it, I'm here to tell you that's complete and utter hogwash. People always find the money for the products and services they really want. Always.

Let me tell you a story to illustrate the point. Back when I was selling real estate, I met with a woman who fell in love with this cute little starter home I was selling. It wasn't very expensive and she had a good job so she could afford the monthly payments. Her problem was she didn't have the down payment. So she left my office and I put her card on the "call back in 3 weeks" pile. I didn't have high hopes for the sale.

Imagine my astonishment when I got an excited call from her a couple days later: "Julia, is that home still available? If so, I want to meet with you this afternoon to sign the paperwork. I got the down payment - I sold my car!!" This woman _sold her car_ to come up with the down payment for this house, because she wanted it that badly.

That experience changed my perception forever about what customers can and cannot afford. If a customer really wants something, they'll find a way to pay for it. So if your customer tells you they can't afford your products and services, you need to take a good hard look in the mirror. Because what they've _really_ just said to you is, "You haven't convinced me I need this."

Having said all that, it's generally easier to sell stuff to people when they don't have to unload their car in order to pay for it. So as a matter of course, it's a good practice to seek out customers who have a little disposable income, so they can more readily say yes to spending some of it on your products and services.

Just don't lull yourself into thinking the reason your business isn't growing is because of the economy, or that times or tough, or people just don't have money these days. Have you seen Apple's sales lately? People have money ... but only for those products and services they _really_ want (or believe they need).

The 3-Step Sales Formula to Maximize Your "Sleaze Appeal"

(Please *do not* try this at home!)

Step #1: *Get your customers to believe they have a problem.* Use scare tactics and hype liberally. Resort when necessary to manipulating what you've learned about their character traits and personality quirks, to get them to experience a sense of irrational fear or even panic, in order to get them to buy.

Step #2: *Make yourself out to be the credible expert they've been seeking.* Feel free to inflate your testimonials, overstate the speed with which you think they'll get results, or even flat-out lie about the features and benefits of what you're selling them - they'll probably never find out anyway!

Step #3: *Make it easy for people to buy.* Offer credit so they're fooled into thinking they can afford something they can't; put all the "fine print" on a separate page where it doesn't distract them from signing; emphasize all the shiny bells and whistles, but forget to mention or discuss the hard work, time or money that will be required of them in order to get the results they're after. Make them think you'll just wave a magic wand (for the right price) and their Big Problem will disappear.

At this point you may be thinking to yourself, "This sounds like exactly the kind of sleazy sales tactics I hate so much! I could never do what you just said, Julia. It would make me a total sleaze-ball!"

I understand why you might think that way. On the surface, the steps I outlined above for changing your customer's beliefs are the exact same sales tactics used by every unethical, manipulative, dirtball salesperson you've ever encountered and don't want to be like.

The critical difference between you and some sleazy salesperson is that not only do you offer products and services that genuinely help people, you're also committed to helping people get those results. Recognizing that powerful fact transforms the sales process from something slimy you do TO your customers, to something authentically helpful you do FOR your customers.

Another point of differentiation between you and a sleazy salesperson is that you recognize the abundance of the Universe. You know that there are more than enough people out there who genuinely need your help; so there's absolutely no need for you force your products and services on somebody who doesn't need or want them.

So when we take the basic 3 steps I outlined above, and now layer in the intention of being authentic and helpful with your customers, we arrive at the 3-Step Sleaze-Free Sales Formula.

The 3-Step Sleaze-Free Sales Formula

1. *Awaken* your customers to the fact that they have a Big Problem.

    Help them see their circumstances in a new way - one that illuminates the Big Problem they're having. Push them when you encounter their resistance to tackle that Big Problem, but only because it's their own fear, doubt and hopelessness that's had them stuck and in pain for so long - and you're here to help them get past all that.

2. **Demonstrate**, with action as well as words, that you are the #1 best person to solve this Big Problem for them.

   Every step of the process with you should demonstrate not just your ability to solve their Big Problem, but also your integrity. You show up on time, you present truthful success stories of previous customers and clients, you acknowledge the limits of your expertise. You even make a recommendation for the customer to talk to to someone other than you, if you determine that you're actually NOT the best person to solve their Big Problem.

3. **Make it simple, easy and painless** for your customers to say "Yes" to taking the next step with you - ie, buying something!

   Explain the entire process thoroughly, including whatever steps they themselves will have to take. Take lots of time with those customers who need it, but be quick and concise with customers who need that from you instead. Describe what you'll do for them and how much it costs, then hand them a pen so they can sign on the dotted line.

The reality is that plenty of potential customers truly need your help. For them to buy and start using your products and services would improve their lives. They would be happier, more fulfilled human beings - or at least they'd have the cleanest carpets ever!

The only reason these potential customers aren't buying from you is they don't know about you. They haven't yet heard (or don't yet fully understand) that you're the one who can help them. In order to fix this for them, **you must sell to them**.

The act of selling your products and services to your customers turns on a light for them. It is this light that lets them finally acknowledge their problems, and wakes them up from living in denial.

You also, by selling to them, give them hope that they no longer have to continue living with their problem. You show them they can live a better life - not only free of their problem, but without any of the pain they might have thought was required in order to fix it.

And most importantly, when you sell to them from an authentic, customer-focused space, you help them to feel supported. *They don't have to do it alone anymore.*

By getting to know you through your sales process, your customers discover that not only are you the perfect person to solve their problems, you're someone they can count on. You'll be there for them, every step of the way. Because they've found you, they're no longer confused, lost, frustrated, searching or hopeless. On the contrary - they're now on the road to a solution!

When all of this is TRUE, and AUTHENTIC, the sales process transforms from something sleazy into something almost spiritual. Because doing your business is what you're here for. It's your mission on this planet, and one that only you can do.

~~~~~~~~~~~~~~~~~~~~~~~~~~~~~~~~~~~

Action Plan - Where are you on the Authentic vs. Sleazy scale?

Re-read the 3 steps of the Sleaze-Free Sales Formula. Now re-read the 3 steps to Maximize Your Sleaze Appeal (in the inset box). Ask yourself honestly where you are currently on each step:

Your customer's problem. Do you even think about your business in terms of the Big Problem you solve for your customers? Or do you use scare tactics and half-truths to trick customers into thinking they need to buy from you?

_____

_____

_____

Your ability to solve your customer's problem. Do you do a good job of demonstrating to your customer that you can solve their problem? Or do you sometimes find yourself resorting to manipulation?

_____

_____

_____

How easy is it for your customer to buy from you? Do you ensure that they fully understand the whole process before signing on the dotted line? Or are you sometimes guilty of hoping they don't ask too many questions?

_____

_____

_____

~~~~~~

In the next chapter, we're going to re-frame the sales process in your mind. Instead of talking about what you sell, we're going to get you talking about how you solve your customer's biggest problem.

And by solving your customer's biggest problem, you instantly get more of your customers saying yes to you than ever before.

... CONTINUE TO THE NEXT CHAPTER ...

Chapter 2: One Simple Step to De-Sleaze Your Entire Sales Process

In the previous chapter, I explained that the first step of the Sleaze-Free Sales Formula is to awaken your customers to the fact that they have a Big Problem, and the second step is to demonstrate how you solve that Big Problem.

These two steps, of course, pre-suppose that you do in fact solve a Big Problem that your customers are having! But do you??

It's critical that you not only solve your customer's Big Problem, but that you _communicate to the customer_ that you solve their Big Problem. Solving your customer's Big Problem is what de-sleazes your entire sales process.

Imagine you just stepped on a big thorn. You're writhing in pain, unable to pull it out yourself. Just then, somebody who specializes in thorn removal walks by. They notice your pain and ask you a few questions. Their approach is empathetic and caring. They understand exactly what your problem is, and are able to fix it.

At this point, you're eager to give them money to fix your problem, and no part of the process has been the slightest bit sleazy.

This is what you want to emulate in your own sales process. And to the extent you do that (and by the end of this book you'll be a pro at it), you will not only be completely sleaze-free, you will also be very, very successful in your business.

"But Julia, my customer doesn't have a simple problem like a thorn sticking out of their foot!"

Are you sure about that? As this chapter goes on to describe, your customer's problems are MUCH simpler than you (the expert) tend to think they are. And the simpler you can make them in your own mind, the more authentically you will connect with your customer.

The Big Problem You Solve vs. What You Do

If you've ever given any thought at all to your marketing, then you've probably thought about what problem it is that you solve. This question of "what problem do you solve?" is Marketing 101, plus it kinda just makes sense, right? If somebody's going to give you money for something, they probably have a problem and they want it fixed.

But most of the time, when I ask a business owner "What problem do you solve?" they tell me what it is that they do, not what problem they solve.

What's the difference, you might ask?

One word: perspective. When you tell a customer what you do, you're seeing YOUR perspective. When you tell your customer what problem you solve, you are seeing your CUSTOMER's perspective.

It's critical that you always see your business from your customer's perspective. Why? Many reasons; but one of the big ones is that your customer's perspective is simple.

Your customer has a clear-cut problem, and they want a clear-cut solution. You may understand the nuances and complexities of both their problem and their solution - and that understanding is exactly why they're going to hire you.

But when you're talking to them about what you're going to do for them, they don't want to hear about all those nuances and complexities. They just want to hear that you have a simple solution to their Big Problem.

All they know, at this early stage, is that they're in pain. Whether it's physical pain, emotional pain, or just the pain of not knowing how to save money on office supplies, they're completely caught up with it. It's an irritant to them, and they want it solved.

Simply. Easily. They do not want to hear all the complexities.

So to get their attention, you must to speak directly to this need - this pain - they're experiencing. In other words, you must precisely identify their Big Problem.

Identifying the Big Problem

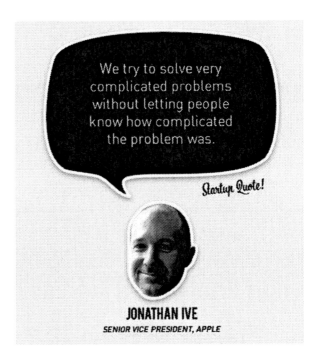

We try to solve very complicated problems without letting people know how complicated the problem was.

Startup Quote!

JONATHAN IVE
SENIOR VICE PRESIDENT, APPLE

When I work with clients privately, I'm able to precisely identify the Big Problem they solve, and shift their perspective from theirs to their customer's. My clients very quickly stop thinking about their sales conversations in terms of what they do, but rather in terms of what their customer needs. And this, in turn, has a dramatic positive impact on their sales results.

But since the limitations of this book prevent me from doing that for you here, I'm going to do the next best thing: I'm going to share with you case studies of numerous clients I've worked with in the past.

By reading about these clients' stories and their transformations, and then by doing the exercise that follows, I trust that you will be able to make big headway in determining the Big Problem that you solve.

"Big Problem" Case Study #1: Tantra Instructor

One of my clients is a Tantra instructor, Charu Morgan, of Embody Tantra in Los Angeles. (To learn more about Charu, please visit http://sleazefreeselling.com/EmbodyTantra)

One of the ways in which she helps people is she teaches them how to unlock the stuck energy in their body through breathing and meditation, so every aspect of their life becomes richer and more dynamic, including their sex life. That is a description of what she does.

But that simple statement of what she does isn't likely to get her customer's attention, right? The reason is because *it doesn't solve a problem*.

Now what if I told you that what she does is she helps you have more satisfying sex? That's a whole lot more compelling, right? Definitely. But why?

First of all, it's a Big Problem. If you're in a relationship and your sex life isn't satisfying, that's something that really sucks. You probably spend a lot of time thinking about it, and wishing there was a solution.

So if you hear somebody say, "I can help you have more satisfying sex," you're going to stop and pay attention.

Another reason the Big Problem she solves is good at catching her customer's attention is that it's stated very clearly. That's an important part of crafting your Big Problem. You don't want a lot of extra words that muddle the point. Extra words are a clue that you're thinking about your own perspective - the solutions you offer. You want to be thinking instead about your customer's perspective - the immediate pain they're in and want fixed.

Finally, and possibly most importantly, the Big Problem that she solves is a compelling one because it's stated in the customer's own language. The person who isn't having a satisfying sex life would say (or at least think to themselves), "I don't have a satisfying sex life."

Some customers might phrase it slightly differently. They might say, "I'm having painful sex;" or "I don't feel an emotional connection with my partner;" but regardless of how they might nuance the problem, the problem of not having satisfying sex is something that the customer themselves would identify.

That's very important when you're looking for The Big Problem that you solve for your customers. It has to be something that they themselves would readily identify. They have to know they have that particular problem.

When Charu wasn't yet seeing the problem she solved through her customers' eyes, she used to say, "I help you to see the blockages of energy you're experiencing in your body. These blockages are causing all kinds of problems, including emotional problems, lack of energy and even sexual dysfunction."

Do you see the difference? A person who's suffering from an unsatisfying sex life would be able to articulate that the root of their problem was energy blockages. They'd be a lot more likely to say, "I'm not having satisfying sex," right? Simple problem.

The energy blockages may in fact be the real cause of their problem, and that's why Charu addresses these blockages when she delivers her solution. But the customer doesn't know that when they first come to her. All they know is they're in pain.

"Big Problem" Case Study #2: Heating & Air Conditioning Contractor

Another client of mine is a father and son team, John and Tom Corcoran, of Corcoran Heating & Air in Chicago. (To learn more about the Corcoran's, please visit http://sleazefreeselling.com/CorcoranHeating)

They have developed advanced technical diagnostics that provide a cutting-edge analysis of your home's heating and air conditioning system. Their tests can identify the equipment that might be outdated, underperforming or even unsafe, then make recommendations for the changes that will be most beneficial for you after 10, 20 or even 50 years of living in your home.

They were actually pretty proud of themselves for having developed that marketing language: "We identify the equipment that might be outdated, underperforming or even unsafe." They really do offer a service that beats out most of their competitors, and that way of describing it spoke to their customer's interests, so that phrase seemed like it would be a compelling way of talking to customers.

But it still wasn't _emotionally_ compelling. It didn't get to the heart of the problem their customer was having - the one that was keeping him up at night.

And what exactly was that problem?

Simply stated, the Corcoran's customer's Big Problem was that they had a room (or an entire floor) of their house that would never get cool enough in the summer, no matter where they set the thermostat.

In the summertime, when the sun was blazing down on the roof all day, it would turn the master bedroom into an oven. Because of the customer's outdated, underperforming or even unsafe air conditioning equipment, they had to crank the air conditioner way up in order to get the bedroom cool enough to sleep in at night. This in turn would turn their first floor or rec room into a walk-in freezer. Plus, they were typically left with astronomical electric bills.

When the Corcoran's started asking their customers, "Do you have one room that never seems to get cool enough, no matter how much money you waste by over air-conditioning the rest of the house?" they saw a much better response rate from their customers.

By addressing their customer's pain point in the form of a succinct Big Problem, they finally found that emotional connection - and sales improvement - they were looking for.

Note: The Corcoran's ultimately stated their Big Problem in the form of a question, and that's a perfectly okay thing to do.

"Big Problem" Case Study #3: Motorcycle Dealership

The last client I want to tell you about is Marty Pavilonis, who owns The Zone Honda Kowasaki motorcycle dealership in Chicago. (To learn more about Marty and The Zone, please visit http://sleazefreeselling.com/TheZone)

At The Zone, Marty sells and services motorcycles, and also sells a wide variety of motorcycle accessories and apparel. While you might be mildly interested in learning more about him - if you liked motorcycles and you happened to live in Chicago - there's not a lot about what I just told you that would make you choose Marty's motorcycle dealership rather than any one of the other motorcycle dealerships in the Chicagoland area.

And in fact, a lot of his competitors have learned this the hard way. Marty's competitors have been going out of business left, right and center during these last few years of economic downturn. When you're having a hard time paying your mortgage, it's not exactly a good time to be shopping for a new bike, right? At least this is the story that his competitors have told themselves about why they're going out of business.

The real reason Marty's competitors have been going out of business is because they all took the old, industry-standard approach to selling motorcycles. They would typically, in their marketing and advertising, talk about their competitive prices, the area's largest selections, and a service team that's the best in the business. This is also the patter their sales teams would use when having one-on-one sales conversations.

But that's an over-used set of promises you might hear from a wide array of businesses, in a variety of industries: a car dealership, a furniture store, or even an electronics big-box store. It's bland, uncompelling and - worst of all

- it fails to address the Big Problem the customer is having.

Think about it: If you're considering buying a motorcycle (or a car, or a stereo, or a recliner for that matter), what's the Big Problem you're trying to solve in your life? I guarantee it's NOT that you have a burning desire for a customer service guy that you can call 24 hours a day. You're also not lying awake at night wondering which store actually has the widest selection, or the lowest prices.

What ARE you concerned about, if you're somebody who might be in the market for a new motorcycle? According to Marty, you simply want more fun in your life!

Marty's big objective, therefore, is to wake them up to the Big Problem in their life. He wants his customer to say, "I'm not having enough fun! I earn good money, I deserve it, and I should be having more fun in my life. So I think I need to buy a motorcycle, that would really solve my problem. I'd have a whole lot more fun."

At this point I'd like to interject a caveat. There are a lot of ways that somebody might solve the Big Problem of not having enough fun in their life, other than by buying a motorcycle. They might go on vacation, sign up for a photography class, or even decide to start dating again.

That's why determining the Big Problem you solve is only the first part of the formula I'm teaching you in this book. In the next chapter, we'll get into some of the other factors you need to take into consideration as well - namely, the type of customer you can best solve problems for.

"Big Problem" Coaching Transcript #1: Relationship Coach

Now let's switch gears away from case studies, and take a look at a coaching conversation I had with a client who was really struggling with determining what Big Problem she solves for her customers.

What I discovered is that Nereida was struggling to identify the Big Problem she solved because she was also having a hard time narrowing down her Ideal Customer - which is the topic of the next chapter. So this conversation with Nereida continues in the following chapter.

Julia: Nereida, what's the Big Problem you solve?

Nereida: I provide healthier and happier relationship communication and interaction.

Julia: OK, that's a clear and concise statement of what you do. But what's the problem that your client has? Would a client come to you and say "I'm in need of happier relationship communication and interaction?"

Nereida: No, they'd say "My relationship with my husband sucks."

Julia: There you go!

Nereida: They'd say, "He screams at me and I have terrible health, and I don't know how to get help with it."

Julia: OK, so that's the problem you solve: "My marriage sucks. I'm unhealthy and I don't know how to get better." Your Ideal Customer is women, right?

Nereida: I get equal both men and women.

Julia: (dubious) You do, really?

Nereida: (emphatically) yes, I do.

Julia: OK. So do the men come to you with the same problem your women do, "My marriage sucks." ?

Nereida: No. They say "I don't know what to do."

Julia: In what capacity, they don't know what to do? About what?

Nereida: When it comes to relationships, in their health and their direction in life. They use the same phrase over and over again about everything: "I just don't know what to do."

Julia: So now I'm going to challenge you to narrow that down a bit. I asked you what it is that they don't know about, and you listed three things: health, relationships and their direction in life. So pick one. What do most men - the highest percentage of those who come to you - what are they concerned about? What's the main thing, for the biggest group of your customers?

As I said before, Nereida was still a little bit confused at this point in our conversation. In the next chapter, when this conversation continues she - and also you - will get more clarity when we dive into understanding who is her Ideal Customer.

~~~~~~~~~~~~~~~~~~~~~~~~~~~~~~~~~~~~~

Action Plan - What's the Big Problem you solve?

Start by stating what you do, in a single sentence, and write it from your own perspective (this is just to get it out of your system):

_____

_____

_____

Now shift to your customer's perspective. What do _they_ say about the problem they're having?

_____

_____

_____

Can you use the above statement, word for word, as the Big Problem you solve? If so, write it below. If not, massage it a little until you're satisfied with it.

(Hint: do NOT use more than 2 lines to write your Big Problem! If you find yourself needing longer, that's a clue card that you're still stuck in your own perspective).

_____

_____

Double-check what you wrote.

Is this in fact a Big Problem? Is it the problem that at least 60% of your customers talk about?

Is it phrased the way your customer would actually say it?

If not, go back to the drawing board!

~~~~~~~~~~~~~~~~~~~~~~~~~~~~~~~~~~~~~~~

If you're having a hard time with this exercise because you're telling yourself that you have different kinds of customers, and they all have different kinds of Big Problems, the next chapter will help you a lot!

... CONTINUE TO THE NEXT CHAPTER ...

Chapter 3: How to Avoid Customers That Bring Out the Sleaze In You

In the previous chapter, we began the work of determining what is the Big Problem you solve for your customer. This is an essential ingredient for both Steps 1 and 2 of the Sleaze-Free Sales Formula.

If you had difficulty narrowing down your Big Problem to a single, concise statement, it's likely because you're gifted at solving a wide range of problems, for a wide range of customers. While you may think that's a good thing, it's actually a significant detriment when it comes to refining your sales and marketing message.

When you try to solve problems for customers who aren't a good fit for you, it's inevitable - they bring out the sleaze in you!

It's one thing to be able to handle a diverse range of problems, when customers who have those problems just happen to walk through your door (and just happen to be ready to pay you). But what we're talking about in this book is how to significantly grow your business by becoming _lots_ better at selling _lots_ more of your products and services.

And trying to sell lots more - when you're not selling by solving Big Problems for the right kinds of customers - will push you into murky, sleazy territory. You'll start using questionable sales tactics, making promises you wish you hadn't made, offering to do things you're not comfortable doing.

So to avoid this sleazy pitfall, you must become skillful at attracting the right kinds of people to you - the people who are suffering to the greatest degree with the problem that you are absolutely best at solving.

These are the people who are most likely to buy from you, without any sleazy sales tactics applied, because they don't need a lot of convincing. They have a thorn in their foot - and you're a thorn-removal specialist!

These people are what's known in marketing lingo as your Ideal Customers.

How do you identify your Ideal Customer?

The absolute best way to determine your Ideal Customer is to carefully analyze who has already bought from you in the past. What you're looking for is commonalities - those traits or characteristics that are shared by a majority of your past customers.

Your initial reaction might be, "But my customers represent a wide spectrum. I've worked with both men and women, from 20 years old to 80, married and single, from a wide geographic region."

That might be true. However, that's not helpful. You need to look for the majority. Unfortunately this is hard for a lot of business owners to do, because by saying "yes" to some people, they are necessarily saying "no" to others.

Sleazy vs Non-Sleazy

The idea of turning away potential customers - just because they don't fit some precise set of criteria - can feel sleazy to some business owners. After all, aren't these people with problems, problems you can solve? And if so, shouldn't you do your very best to help them solve them?

Definitely not. When you get to Part 2 of this book and begin implementing these new Sleaze-Free tactics in your business, you'll see that your sales and marketing efforts are much more efficient when you're able to focus as narrowly as possible on certain kinds of customers. If you skip the step of narrowing down your Ideal Customer, you'll be working a lot harder down the road, for smaller returns. In other words, you'll be wasting time on ineffective sales and marketing, and thus having less time to do what you love - serve customers!

To push yourself through this process, keep telling yourself that saying "no" to some types of customers means that you will be able to say "yes" to many more.

The customers you'll be saying "no" to, remember, are less than ideal for you. They might be good people, and they might be really suffering with something you could help them with. But there are other people who are suffering more, from problems you can help more with. To say nothing of the fact that when you give your help to only your Ideal Customers, your business is easier and more profitable.

And you only get to say "yes" to all of those Ideal Customers by saying no to the less than ideal ones.

The following case studies and coaching transcripts will further illuminate this process.

"Ideal Customer" Case Study #1: Tantra Instructor

My client Charu and I have been able to identify that her best customer is somebody who has problems in their sex life and they're highly motivated to want to fix them.

They might be experiencing a specific issue, such as painful sex or lack of intimacy. Or, they might be desiring sex that's more titillating. But bottom line, they're having unsatisfying sex, and they really want to change that!

However, the desire for more satisfying sex is only part of the story for Charu's Ideal Customers.

Her Ideal Customer is also on a spiritual path. While they do desire an improvement in their sex lives, they view it as part of the larger picture of becoming a better person and transforming their soul. For them, more satisfying sex is an integral part of walking their spiritual path in life. Some have a desire for sex that is so great, it transcends the body and becomes a spiritual experience.

It's very important whenever Charu and I are talking about marketing messages, that we not emphasize the desire for better sex and forget about the spiritual transformation her Ideal Customer also desires. Similarly, we can't focus on the spiritual transformation that's possible through tantra, without discussing the sexual experiences that will get you there.

We always have to keep in mind both, because her customer is somebody who is concerned about both.

<u>Exercise</u>

What's the desired outcome of your customer?

"Ideal Customer" Case Study #2: Heating & Air Conditioning Contractor

My heating and air conditioning client, the Corcoran's, need to keep in mind that their Ideal Customer must meet a number of criteria.

First of all, their Ideal Customer is affluent because their solution is not an inexpensive one. But beyond that, the Big Problem that they are addressing is one of _comfort_ - and affluent people are much more inclined to pay for comfort than non-affluent people are.

Secondly, their Ideal Customer lives in a multi-story house. Why? Because the Big Problem they identified is that one room is uncomfortably warm, even while the rest of the house is icy. And this phenomenon is most likely to occur in a multi-story house.

Does this mean they won't work with people who call them up and who happen to live in a ranch-style home, or even a single-story condo? No, of course not.

But what it does mean is that when they're creating marketing campaigns, they don't think about the three calls they happened to get this past week from people who happen to own ranch-style homes. Rather, they must continually remind themselves that their Ideal Customer lives in a multi-story house, because they're the ones with the Big Problem they can most readily and impressively solve.

The Corcoran's also need to remember that their Ideal Customer is someone who's married, or at least living together. While certainly they would take a service call from someone who lives alone, the Big Problem they solve assumes that there are multiple people living in the house: one who doesn't mind it a little warmer, another one who insists upon having it nice and cool. It's this situation of two people always wanting two different temperatures that causes the friction - the Big Problem - that the Corcoran's can now swoop in and solve.

In other words, if there was a man living all by himself (and I'm being very stereotypical here - good marketing depends upon looking at the norm), he might be willing to sleep in a hotter bedroom. Or, on a really hot night he would go sleep on the couch in the family room, which is the room that's overly air conditioned.

With either one of these stop-gaps, this single man's problem would be solved, and he would no longer have the Big Problem that the Corcoran's could solve for him.

Conversely, the divorced woman living by herself might just crank the air conditioning more and more and more, rather than thinking there might be a technical or engineering solution (again, we're going with stereotypical norms here - please spare me the hate mail about how you're a single woman who owns her own toolbox!)

The woman living by herself can overlook the freezing-cold family room, or justify the high electrical bill as a "necessity" in order to make the temperature in her bedroom comfortable.

As these two examples illustrate, it's the fact that there's two people living together (typically married) that creates the friction of the Big Problem that the Corcoran's solve. One is comfortable and the other is cold; if the second one is warm enough the other is boiling up. And neither one thinks that the other person's solution is acceptable.

When thinking about their Ideal Customer, therefore, the Corcoran's must not get swayed into thinking about single people, or city dwellers, or people who aren't affluent. They might be able to help them, yes; but focusing on them, when they're designing their marketing campaigns, won't help them grow their business.

Exercise

What conditions must be present in order for you to work your special brand of magic

on your customer's Big Problem?

_____

_____

_____

"Ideal Customer" Case Study #3: Motorcycle Dealership

The most important characteristic Marty needs to keep in mind is that his Ideal Customers are male. But that's an easy one for him, which he never forgets. He knows very clearly that his best customer is a man.

Not that women don't buy motorcycles, but women don't tend to buy motorcycles _from him_. It doesn't matter, for the purpose of this exercise, why that is - but Marty knows from years of sales data that it just happens to be true. And that's what's important to focus on when identifying his Ideal Customer.

If he decides for some reason he wants to expand into the women's market, that's fine. But that will require an entirely different approach than selling to his existing market, which is men.

In looking at Marty's past customers, it's also obvious that his typical customer thinks of himself as somewhat of a rebel. It makes sense, right? A guy who's kind of square - like an accountant type, or the kind of guy who much prefers to do crossword puzzles for fun - is not the guy that's going to think it's fun to ride a motorcycle, much less buy one.

This aspect of his Ideal Customer's personality is a little harder for Marty to remember because while he himself is also a bit of a rebel, he doesn't necessarily see himself that way. So it's easy for him to forget that his customers are rebels too.

He sees himself as a business owner, and a smart guy and a good member of the community and all that. While that's all true, he's also a guy who thinks that motorcycles are the best way to have fun!! He forgets that he himself is quite a bit of a rebel and that a lot of men who want to have fun aren't like him, and they would choose something other than a motorcycle if they decided it was time to have more fun in their life.

It's important for him to remember to continually appeal to that rebel side of his customer in his marketing. He can't go after just straight laced business owners; nor can he go after ordinary guys who are just living in the suburbs raising a family.

He's got to go for the men who have that rebel streak - the ones who like to party, who chafe a little bit at rules, and who are proud of that part of their personality - because they're the ones who want to buy a motorcycle in order to bring more fun into their lives.

<u>Exercise</u>

In what ways do you represent your own Ideal Customer?

_____

_____

_____

Now we're going to switch gears and study a few conversations I've had with clients. This will show you the thought and questioning process that you need to go through as you're identifying your Ideal Customer, and eliminating those customers who don't fit all your criteria.

"Ideal Customer" Coaching Transcript #1: Mortgage Broker

Julia: Michelle, let's hear about your Ideal Customer.

Michelle: That would be a homeowner with good credit, looking for one on one service.

Julia: OK, is there anything else that we can say about them? Do they own a $200,000 home or a $1,000,000 home? Does that matter?

Michelle: Ideally I would say someone that owes anywhere from $300,000 to $400,000 would be my ideal client.

Julia: OK, great, that's really good to know. Somebody who has a moderate income, but they're not wealthy.

Michelle: Right.

Julia: There's one thing you didn't mention in your description of your Ideal Customer, and that is the reason they're looking for a loan. Is that important?

Michelle: They probably have a higher rate than what they think they should have.

Julia: And does it matter to you how long they've been in their home?

Michelle: Yes. I'll say at least two years.

Julia: Great. So they've nested a bit, but they haven't put down deep roots.

Michelle: Yes.

Julia: And what about their marital status?

Michelle: It doesn't matter.

Julia: Are you sure? It may not matter as far as your ability to do a loan for them, but if you look over the last 25 customers you've had, has there been a pattern?

Michelle: You know, I think you're right. The majority of people who call me are women. Sometimes they turn out to be married so I'm doing the loan for the couple, but the person who actually reaches out first is almost always the woman.

Julia: Great! The reason that's so important is because there could be something in the way you present yourself that you are not even aware of, that tends to attract women more so than men.

And once you become aware of that, you can turn up the volume on that aspect of yourself, so that you become even more effective at attracting the kinds of people who will say yes to you - which you've said is women.

Even though by law you can't say you'll only give a loan to somebody if they're a man or a woman or married or whatever, by looking at the last twenty five people you've actually worked with, you get a lot of information about who you attract.

Exercise

Are there customers you _could_ work with, but who don't happen to call you very much? Identify them; and then eliminate them from your Ideal Customer description.

"Ideal Customer" Coaching Transcript #2: Graphic Designer & Marketing Consultant

Julia: Deborah, tell me about your ideal client.

Deborah: Most of my customers are non-profits. And the people I interact with at these organizations are the kind of people who want to help other people. A lot of them are female. They're civic minded, they're change-the-world sort of types, but not in the radical way. And a lot of times they're PhDs or at least have Masters degrees, and they're Liberal Arts majors.

And their pain problem is they just want great looking documents and printed materials. I don't think they understand anything about marketing, but they get really thrilled when it looks great.

Julia: That is so great, Deborah. That is a really rich well of information that you've been able to identify about your Ideal Customer. There's a number of things that are really juicy in there that we can work with.

You know that your people are mostly women, they have advanced degrees and they really like marketing materials that look good. You also said they're kind of civic minded. I would actually venture a guess, that if we dove down a little bit more, that your Ideal Customers are probably aging hippies?

Deborah: Yeah, some of them, yeah.

Julia: So you know they are the ones who were seventeen years old in 1967, right?

Deborah: Mm-hm.

Julia: Many of those people still have those value systems of the late 60s and early 70s. They're intellectual, very intelligent, and while they're probably motivated by words, they also have an artistic sensibility that makes them motivated by images and graphics.

Deborah: Yeah.

Julia: So all of that is wonderful that you have such a rich understanding of who your Ideal Customer. It's also important to understand that you're looking for the more creative type.

Deborah: Yeah.

Julia: This helps you to understand that the CEOs and decision makers you attract are creative and visionary. Not only is that the type of person you enjoy being with, but also down the road when you're talking about marketing methods, you want to talk about yourself as the artist. Because that's what's going to speak to them -- the artist part of them even if they're business owners. You get that?

Deborah: Yeah, right. [Laughter]

Exercise

Once you know some facts about who your Ideal Customer is, what are some

conclusions you can draw about their personalities or background?

_____

_____

_____

"Ideal Customer" Coaching Transcript #3: Relationship Coach

This conversation is a continuation from the conversation that we started back in Chapter 2, where Nereida was struggling to identify her Big Problem because she was also confused about who her Ideal Customer is.

What we ultimately discovered together is that while her Ideal Customers are both men and women, they each have a distinct Big Problem she solves. In this conversation, we drilled down to some of the specifics about her Ideal Customer.

Julia: Nereida, how are you coming with narrowing down your Ideal Customer?

Nereida: Okay. I attract men who are very overwhelmed with life -- stressed out thinking that they're not in control of everything that's going on. And I attract women who feel unfulfilled in their relationships.

Julia: Okay, so let's focus first on the women. Is it women who are unfulfilled primarily with their romantic relationship? As opposed to the other kinds of relationships in their life?

Nereida: I would say, 75%, yes. I do get some who have issues with children ...

Julia: Okay, but again, we're going for the majority with this exercise, so let's stay focused on the women who are unsatisfied with their romantic relationship. And these are women who are unsatisfied with their marriages, or do you attract women who are in dating relationships and unsatisfied with their boyfriends?

Nereida: Marriages.

Julia: Wonderful, that's a great distinction to make. So we can leave aside unmarried women for now, right?

Nereida: Uh-huh.

Julia: Okay, fabulous. Is there a pattern as far as how long they've been married? Five years, twenty years, one year?

Nereida: Ten and up.

Julia: Great. So we're looking at people who been married for a long time and are not satisfied. Is there any particular pattern of dysfunction going on? One that you mentioned was screaming.

Nereida: Screaming or just total ... they don't acknowledge each other.

Julia: Okay, so when I say particular patterns of dysfunction, what I want you to look for is specific things showing up like they're not having sex anymore, they're fighting about money, they disagree about how to raise the kids ...

Nereida: They're not interacting, they're not having sex anymore. When they do interact, it's negative. He's not around.

Julia: Okay, he's not around. Great. So that leads me to my next question, has one or both of them had an affair?

Nereida: You mean the woman having an affair?

Julia: Either.

Nereida: Okay, the women that I worked with have not had affairs. And whether the man has or not, I would not know, they do not -- the wives would not -- they wouldn't know. They don't tell me. That's not something we talk about.

Julia: Okay, great. So we leave that out of the equation. But it's good to know that they have not themselves had affairs, so they're loyal, they're committed to the marriage. Which also leads me to believe also that they are not highly sexually motivated because if they were, they would be having an affair, so they want something other than sex as their primary means of getting fulfilled.

Nereida: Yes. They're mostly dedicated to their marriage because it's a lifestyle they have become accustomed to - not necessarily because they even like the man anymore.

Julia: Okay, so that's getting even deeper into the problem that you solve.   Ultimately are you coaching them to have the strength to leave their husband and go find a more fulfilling life?

Nereida: Ultimately, I'm coaching them to figure out do they want to stay or not. And if they do stay, which I call Option A, what do they need to change in order to make their marriage fulfilling again. Or if they decide they want to leave, that's Option B, we talk about how they can do that too.

Julia: All right, great. Let's project into the future a bit, and if you discover with further analysis of your past customers that a large percentage of the women you work with actually do end up choosing option A, now you can talk very openly in your marketing about how great option A is.

Keep in mind that as you do that, you'll be alienating the women who really in their hearts know they want to take Option B. However, you'll be speaking so deeply to the women who really do want option A - who are the majority of your customers anyway - that it won't matter for you. Because that's ultimately the goal - to get so crystal clear about what your Ideal Customer really wants, that you're able to talk just to that person and turn away the people who aren't good clients for you anyway.

Nereida: Okay.

<u>Exercise</u>

If you really do have two groups of Ideal Customers (but don't allow yourself any more than two!), in what ways do they have different Big Problems?

_____

_____

_____

It is absolutely critical that you begin to narrow the pool of people you regard as Ideal Customers. And hopefully these examples have helped you see that.

This may be difficult for some of you because by definition you're leaving out some segment of your customers. And a lot of you think of your customers as your children almost: they've got problems, and you want to help them!

Also you feel like you are a good problem solver and you can solve lots of different problems for lots of different kinds of people, and you don't want to limit yourself.

But the whole point with clarity is to really, really focus on who is your _best_ customer, and then put all your effort into acquiring more of those. You can always go back later and branch out - but for the following exercise I want you to go for the middle.

~~~~~~

Action Plan - Who is your Ideal Customer?

Write down the names of either your best customers, or your last 25 customers. This could be the customers who have spent the most with you, the ones who buy from you most frequently, or those who are your best referral sources (In fact, you get bonus points if you make 3 separate lists for those 3 categories!)

_____

_____

_____

_____

_____

_____

Now ask yourself questions to help you identify common traits among these people. Easy ones to start with are age, gender, marital status, etc. Use the conversations I've described in the six previous examples to help you.

What age do my Ideal Customers tend to be?

_____

Are they male or female?

_____

Are they married or single?

What do I know about my customers' personalities?

_____

_____

_____

What do they want out of life? (this starts to speak to the Big Problem they want solved, or the types of solutions that will be most attractive to them)

_____

_____

_____

If you skipped any of the Exercises that were scattered throughout the Case Studies and Coaching Transcripts, go back and answer those questions.

Now that you've got a very clear idea of who your Ideal Customer is, go through your original list of 25 names and draw a line through the people who don't fit this new description of your Ideal Customer. Ouch! Is that painful?

Keep in mind you're not actually eliminating this person from the face of the earth - you're not even saying that you'll no longer work with that person.

All you're doing is recognizing that that's not the kind of customer you want to attract more of in the future.

~~~~~~~~~~~~~~~~~~~~~~~~~~~~~~~~~~~~

Having trouble? Ask me a question!

If you're having difficulty with this exercise and want help, please visit http://juliakline.com/members/ask-a-question/. On that website, you can submit a question and get an answer from me, personally, within 24 hours!

This is a limited time offer, to help promote this book. Eventually the page - and the chance to ask questions - will no longer be available free of charge. So go there now!

~~~~~~~~~~~~~~~~~~~~~~~~~~~~~~~~~~~~

Even after you've identified the Big Problem you solve (in Chapter 2) and started talking to your Ideal Customers about that problem (in Chapter 3), you know that prospective customers don't always say yes. And trying to get them to say yes, or "close" them, is exactly what leaves so many business owners feeling downright sleazy! (and leaves your customers running the other way whenever they see you)

But of course, your customers MUST say "yes" to you - and you must get good at getting them to say yes ...

... because if you don't, you go out of business.

The next chapter will help you to master the part of the sales process known as "overcoming objections," or getting your customers to say yes. And you'll learn to do it in a way that is truly helping and supporting your customers, so neither you nor they leave the conversation feeling sleazy.

... CONTINUE TO THE NEXT CHAPTER ...

Chapter 4: Turning "No" Into "Yes" ... The Non-Sleazy Way

This may be hard for you to hear, but your customers often believe very little of what you tell them. You've told them your Whammo 9000 is the best on the market and it will solve their Big Problem, but still they don't buy.

Why don't they buy?

In short, it's because many of your potential customers don't believe what you've said. They don't think the Whammo 9000 is the best on the market, and they certainly don't believe it will solve their Big Problem.

And if your customers don't believe you, you can't accomplish the 3-Step Sleaze-Free Sales Formula, and grow your business:

1. ***Awaken*** your customers to the fact that they have a Big Problem.

2. ***Demonstrate***, with action as well as words, that you are the #1 best person to solve this Big Problem for them.

3. ***Make it simple, easy and painless*** for your customers to say "Yes" to taking the next step with you - ie, buying something!

In marketing lingo, this lack of belief is what we call "customer objections" and they are the bane of every salesperson's existence. This chapter is all about how to get customers to believe you, and thus "overcome their objections" so they start to say yes to you.

But before you can overcome any objections, or awaken any customers to their problems, you have to know what those problems are. And how do you do that? Simple - you ask them.

Of course you can't simply ask, "Why don't you want to buy?" because that will cause your customer to offer a bunch of excuses. You'll be no closer to knowing their real reasons for not buying than you were.

Rather you need to ask a variety of probing questions that gets your customer talking about their problem. As they talk, listen carefully. Don't assume you know the reasons behind the reasons; instead, ask followup questions.

Eventually, with practice, you will begin to understand what's really going on for your customers - and the real reasons they're not buying from you. Only then can you help them to change their mind, and buy from you after all.

Sleazy vs. Non-Sleazy

Bear in mind, we're not trying to trick anybody into anything. As you'll read below, becoming skillful at overcoming objections simply allows you to help customers get over their own resistance, hopelessness and fear. In doing so, they're now able to say "yes" to a solution of yours that will help them live a better life.

But if, during the sales process, you realize that the customer doesn't in fact have a Big Problem or that it's a Big Problem that's outside your personal area of expertise, then the ethical thing to do is to thank them for their time and end the conversation.

Step 1: Awaken Your Customer To Their Problem

If your customer doesn't think they have a problem, then it's going to be pretty tough for you to sell them anything at all. Because if they don't have a problem to solve, what are you going to do for them?

That's why awakening your customer to the fact that they do, in fact, have a problem is Step One of the 3-Step Sleaze-Free Sales Formula.

<u>I don't have a Problem</u>

Let's go through a number of different variations of what your customer might be thinking - or saying - when their objection boils down to, "I don't think I have a problem." Following that, I'll discuss a number of methods for truthfully awakening them to this Big Problem of theirs.

<u>Variation 1</u>:   "I have a problem, but I don't need help with it. I can fix it by myself."

The way that you overcome this objection in your marketing is to list for them all of the things that they have probably done on their own to try and fix the problem.

This will show that you really understand them -- you get them, you know they want to do it by themselves, and you understand all the different solutions they've already tried that didn't work. But you know their dirty little secret - that despite their best efforts, they're still living with this problem. "So really, Mr. or Mrs. Customer, don't you think that it might be time for help?"

<u>Variation 2</u>: "I'm in no rush to fix it. I can live with this problem for a while."

In marketing lingo, we say that a customer like this doesn't have any urgency. So your job is to create that sense of urgency!

There are typically two methods for creating urgency: 1) turn up the pain on what they're experiencing because of their Big Problem, and ask them how much longer they're willing to live with this now-excruciating pain.

The second method is the opposite: 2)   Paint a tantalizing picture of what their life could be like if they weren't suffering with this Big Problem, and ask them how many more days of their life they are willing to waste, living a less fulfilling life than they could?

<u>Variation 3</u>: "I've already got a guy. He handles this stuff for me, so I don't have a problem with it."

This can show up in a bunch of different ways. It could be, "I've always been satisfied with who I'm using now." If that's the objection you get, then you somehow need to demonstrate that the same old guy they've been using forever might not be up to the minute on the newest innovations in your industry, but you are.

Another variation is, "The person I use now is convenient and I think that you'll be inconvenient." This could show up as, "My guy brings my papers to my office" or "my guy offers overnight delivery." So naturally what you need to do is demonstrate that you're also convenient. But make sure that you don't bend over backward and all of a sudden be inconveniencing yourself   just to land a customer.

A third variation on that is, "The person I use now sends referrals my way and I don't want to lose that." One way to deal with that objection is to ask whether or not that's really true. They might have the story in their head that they get all these referrals from their accountant, but really really does their accountant sends them referrals? Maybe not. Maybe one time he sent him a really great referral, but hasn't sent him any other referrals in years. The other approach, of course, is to demonstrate that you also can send them referrals.

Another variation is, "The person I use now is s a friend or a relative and I don't want to damage that relationship." Your best approach in this situation is to come up with a creative way that they can continue working with the friend or relative and just squeeze you in a little bit on the side. And then once you've got your foot in the door, of course, you can bust it open and start taking on larger and larger pieces of work.

A last variation is "I'm getting a great price from whoever I'm using now, and I don't believe that you can beat it or match it." That is one that I want you to walk away from. Trying to be the lowest-price guy in town is a battle you're never going to win - somebody will always come along who's willing to the job cheaper. Plus, it's pretty tough to make a living when you're scraping by on minimal profit margin.

<u>Overcoming Denial</u>

A lot of times when your customer doesn't think they have a problem, they're simply in denial. They think, "Well, my situation isn't great, but it's fine for now."

An example of this is people who say to themselves, "I'm a few pounds overweight, but it's no big deal, it's fine, I'm okay with it."

And in this case, what you need to do is awaken them to the idea that, no, it's not fine, this is a huge problem and it's getting worse by the minute. If you don't address it now, you will have some really Big Problems on your hands in a very short time.

Do this by showing pictures - literally or figuratively - of other people who have this same problem. Do it in such a way that they will recognize themselves in these other people.

Illuminating the Real Problem

Another reason why they don't think they have a problem is because they're convinced their problem is different than it really is.

Recently I talked to an attorney who told me he didn't have time to write a weekly newsletter. However, that's not his real problem. The real problem is he's wasting hours a week on unnecessary tasks. If he streamlined his client intake process, he would find himself with plenty of extra hours to do more effective marketing. But he is convinced that his problem is that he doesn't have the time to write a newsletter.

If that's the case with your customers, your job is to tell them stories about other people just like them who are similarly deluded and provide helpful clues that reveal the real problem.

Simplify the Problem

Another reason why they don't think that they have a problem is they think, "I'm not really sure exactly what my problem is or what the steps are that are required to fix it, so I would rather just do nothing."

A good example of this kind of denial is a homeowner who's facing a foreclosure. They might think to themselves, "I really don't know what's going on. I don't understand all this legal mumbo-jumbo, I don't know what my rights are, I don't know what my options are, I don't know how much time I have. In short, I don't know what I need to do to fix the problem, so I'm going to stick my head in the sand and just hope that this whole thing blows over."

That's a very dangerous version of "I don't think that I have a problem," yet it happens all the time in lots of industries.

Your best approach in that case is to educate them. Not only does it help them get closer to embracing their Big Problem, but it also paints you as the expert. In other words, it's begins to accomplish Step 2 of the Sleaze-Free Formula, "Demonstrate that you can solve their problem."

Make sure to keep the education process simple. Don't let yourself get caught up in complexities and nuances. Stay focused on the most basic explanations of both their problem and its solution - making sure to demonstrate that the solution is actually simpler than they think it is.

Show Them What "Normal" Is (without the problem)

Another objection is that they genuinely don't realize that the problem that they're living with isn't normal.

The example that comes to my mind is on the TV show Friends, when Chandler needs to get measured for pants. So Joey tells Chandler, "Go to my guy, I've been going to him since I was a little kid, he'll measure you for pants. He's great."

So Chandler goes to the tailor, but when he measures his inseam, the tailor gives him a quick fondle in the crotch! Yikes! NOT what he was wanting from a tailor.

The next day when Joey sees Chandler, he asks him, "Hey, how do you like my tailor? He's pretty great, right?" And Chandler says, "No, Joey, he's not great. In fact, your tailor is a bad, bad man!"

He then relates the story of what happened and Joey says, "What are you talking about? That's how you measure pants." And Chandler has to tell him, "No, Joe, that is not how you measure pants!"

Sometimes, like Joey, your customer might be experiencing a Big Problem, but honestly not know that it's a problem. They might just think it's normal.

A more real-world example would be someone who gets a headache every single afternoon of their life. They might have lived with it for so long that they truly don't realize that that shouldn't be happening.

If this is your customer, you need to tell them stories of other people who are in the same situation. Describe the situation, the symptoms, the thought process in such a way that the customer can recognize himself.   Then gently point out that this is not normal, it's actually a Big Problem - one you can fix.

<u>Some Customers Don't Have a Problem</u>

One final possibility when someone tells you they don't have a problem, is that perhaps they actually don't have the problem that you're offering to solve. In that case, what you need to do is look for a different customer.

That might seem obvious, but sometimes (especially if you're in the scrapper, business-building phase when every new customer is precious to you), you can be tempted to just keep barking up the wrong tree. Or worse, attempt to convince somebody to buy something even though you know they don't need what you're selling. Because that would in fact make you a sleaze-ball!

Step 2: Demonstrate Their Problem Can Be Solved

Step #2 of the Sleaze-Free Sales Formula is to demonstrate that you are the #1 best person to solve their problem for them.

This is typically the most difficult part of the sales process - not because you're not good at what you do, and not even because the customer doesn't believe that you are.

Rather, customers often feel hopeless that their problem can be solved at all, and that's why they don't buy. No matter what you say they don't believe you - not because they have any doubts about you or your ability, but simply because of their own sense of hopelessness.

When this is the case, your customer's discouragement, frustration and unwillingness to buy has a lot more to do with themselves than anything you did or didn't do.

You know this is what's going on for your customer if they say things like, "I've talked to some many other experts, it's hopeless. I'm destined to suffer with this problem forever."

Or in some cases they think that success depends upon their own action and in the past they've disappointed themselves, so now they think that they can't take the necessary action and solve their problem.

That's a big one for weight loss businesses, right? The customer thinks to themselves, "I know I need to get some exercise and stop eating so much if I'm ever going to lose this weight. But I'm not willing to do either one of those things, so there's no way I can lose weight. It's hopeless, I'm not even going to try."

In other cases, their lack of belief in themselves is deeply ingrained in their psyche. Something like, "I'm not just not any good at Math, so I'm not even going to try to balance my finances. I guess I'm destined for bankruptcy / foreclosure / crushing debt."

If your customer is feeling hopeless, for whatever reason, your job in that case is to restore a spark of hope.

Restore Hope Tactic #1: Paint the Picture

One way to restore that spark of hope is to reinforce how great it would be if by some miracle this problem actually went away. A lot of the diet commercials take this approach when they show you testimonials of person after person who says "Nothing ever worked before, but this new approach was different because of XYZ. And it turned out that XYZ was the twist that finally worked for me to reach my goal weight."

An approach like that wears down the customer's psyche and they start thinking, "Oh, God, I would love to be skinny. Wouldn't that be sooo great. Maybe XYZ will be the twist that finally works for me, too." And that desire begins to slowly overshadow the voice that has been saying, "No, it's never going to work. I've tried this before. I'm doomed for failure."

By wearing them down, you finally inspire them to take action - action that will solve their problem.

<u>Restore Hope Tactic #2: Shift Responsibility Away From the Customer</u>

There's another approach you can take, if your customer's problem is that they don't have any confidence in their own ability to make the changes necessary to get the results they want. And that is to shift responsibility off of themselves and put it onto something external.

Weight Watchers employs this tactic when they say,"You don't have to stop eating, you just have to count your points." Because while the customer may in the past have tried (and failed) to cut back on calories, she's never tried counting points before. So her brain starts saying, "Hey this Points thing just might work," so she gives it a try.

(And guess what - if she succeeds at counting Points, she will succeed at losing weight! So it's not only an effective marketing strategy, it's also one that has the potential of creating a lot of positive results for Weight Watchers' customers.)

A great way for a lot of businesses to shift the responsibility off the customer and onto something external is to offer done-for-you services.

When you offer done-for-you services, you're saying to your customer, "You don't need to worry about XYZ, I'll do that for you." So for example if you were a marketing person you might tell your customer, "This website that I'm going to design, or this copy that I'm going to write, will be so good that you don't need to worry about whether or not you (or your salespeople) are actually any good at selling your product."

You take the burden off them, and put it onto something external - namely, you and your product or service.

Restore Hope Tactic #3: Offer a Guarantee

A guarantee is also very useful at overcoming hopelessness.   Your customer might be completely convinced that your solution won't actually work; but they figure they've got nothing to lose, so they might as well give it a shot. So they buy - and now you've got your chance to show them your solution DOES work!

In this situation you don't want to shy away from big claims like "Lose 15 lbs in two weeks or get your money back" because all you're trying to do is to get them to buy your product or service.   Even if they don't lose 15 pounds, but they lose 5 pounds, they're still going to be thrilled and won't return the product - even if it didn't technically deliver on the guarantee.

Note: If you're a U.S. company the Federal Trade Commission might have a lot to say about what you can and cannot promise in your guarantee. So like I said in my disclaimer at the beginning of this book - I'm not a lawyer, so don't take any legal advice from me. Hire a lawyer!

Step 3: Make the Solution Easy

Strangely enough, a real fear that a lot of customers have is, "I don't want you to fix my problem, because the cure might actually be worse than the problem." Fortunately this is a relatively easy objection to handle, once you know it's what you're dealing with.

> In our weight loss example, the customer would say, "I want to lose weight, but to do that I'd have to stop eating. And the idea of denying myself food is worse than the problem of being overweight."

> If your business is as a web designer, your customers might think to themselves, "I'm sure that you can build me a fabulous website, but it's probably going to cost me $15,000 and I'm not willing to do that." Before even getting a quote!

> If the Big Problem you're addressing is a relationship concern, they might be thinking to themselves, "The fact of the matter is my relationship sucks. My husband's never going to change, so if you start helping me, I'm going to realize that what I have to do is get divorce, I'm not willing to do that."

If any of these concerns are in play for your customer, your job is to show them that the cure is only a short term pain. Help them believe that it will be like ripping off the Band-Aid - a short burst of pain that ultimately clears the way for long-term solution.

Alternatively, you can demonstrate that what they fear is actually not going to come to pass or won't be as bad as they think it will.

Examples of this approach are: "You probably don't have to get divorced, you're just going to identify a few little things that need to be renegotiated." Or "No, it's not going to cost $15,000 for a new website, it might only cost $7,500." By showing them that their fears are not as bad as they thought they were, you get them into a frame of mind where they're ready to buy.

~~~~~~~~~~~~~~~~~~~~~~~~~~~~~~~~~~~~

Action Plan - Why isn't your customer buying?

This has been an extremely meaty chapter, one you might spend hours, days or even weeks working through. This question of "Why isn't my customer buying?" is not always easy to discover.

Look back over the last 5 potential customers who told you "no." What was each of their reasons? (If you think their reason was "I can't afford it," go deeper. That's never the real reason.)

_____

_____

_____

What questions (and followup questions) can you ask
your customers to get them talking about their real
reasons for not buying?

_____

_____

_____

Do your customers think they don't have a problem? If
so, which variation do they talk about most often? What
can you say to awaken them to their Big Problem?

_____

_____

_____

Do your customers think their Big Problem can't be
solved?   If not, why not?   What can you say to
demonstrate that you can help them solve it.

_____

_____

_____

~~~~~~

Congratulations! You've gotten to the end of Part I of this book, Laying the Foundation. You should, by now, have a very clear idea of how you serve your customers with the products and services you sell. And more importantly, you should feel comfortable with - even enthusiastic about - talking to them about buying those products and services.

But how do you do more of the actual selling, without slipping back into Sleaze-ville? First you need people to talk to; and then you need something specific to talk to them about. To get those two things in an authentic, non-sleazy way, keep reading.

... CONTINUE TO THE NEXT CHAPTER ...

Part 2: Turning the Sleaze-Free Sales Formula into Cash

Chapter 5: How to Get All the Customers You'll Ever Need

In the first 4 chapters of this book, I explained the marketing foundation you need to have in place in order for the Sleaze-Free Sales Formula to work for you. Did you do the exercises throughout each chapter, and the Action Plans at the end? If you did, then this is what you've accomplished so far:

- In Chapter 2, you defined the Big Problem you solve for your customers - the one that makes prospects stop and listen to what you have to say.
- In Chapter 3, you discovered whose problems you are best at solving - these are your Ideal Customers. These are the people who are _most likely to say yes_ to working with you - so you want to attract them, more than anyone else.
- In the last chapter, Chapter 4, you developed strategies to help your customers overcome their own doubt, hopelessness and fear (otherwise known in marketing lingo as "overcoming objections.") So instead of hearing "I'll think about it," or "I'll get back to you," you start hearing a lot of "Yes! I'd like to start working with you right now."

As much work as that was, you've only accomplished half the battle. You've Laid the Foundation. And laying the foundation doesn't pay the bills!

In order to grow your business and live the life you've always dreamed of living (not simply "pay the bills,") you need to reach - and sell to - lots more people than you have before.

Reaching - and selling to - many more potential customers is what Part 2 of this book covers:

- Here in Chapter 5, we're going to discuss methods for acquiring customers - known in marketing lingo as Lead Generation. Because in order to make sales, you need people to sell to!
- Chapter 6 shows you how to approach these potential customers without feeling like a sleaze-ball. Marketers call this part of the sales process "making an offer" - and it's the part of traditional sales that most often feels sleazy, because it's where you're asking them to buy from you. But when you follow my prescription for how to make your offer, you'll turn that feeling of sleaziness around. Now both you and your customers will look forward to the part where you ask them to buy from you.
- Chapter 7 ensures that you never again let a single sale slip through your fingers. It does this by outlining simple, authentic strategies for following up over time with all the potential customers who didn't say yes to you right away.

By the time you've finished with the rest of this book, you'll have a systematized process for approaching new customers, inviting them to do business with you, and then following up with both your yes's and your no's, so that not a single sale ever slips through your fingers again.

In short, Part 2 of this book teaches you how to turn the Sleaze-Free Sales Formula into cash!

Sleazy vs. Non-Sleazy

The process of finding customers to talk to is what we marketers call "generating a lead," or lead gen, for short.

You can generate a lead ...

- Online. By asking someone to fill out their name and email address in exchange for something they want - a video, a free report, etc.

- Through the mail. By sending a postcard or flyer or letter that asks the customer to "call, click or stop by."

- Via print or broadcast advertising. By telling the reader or listener or viewer to do something that will result in you capturing their contact information.

- In person. Typically by exchanging business cards.

There are dozens, if not hundreds, of specific strategies for generating leads, and I spend the majority of this chapter detailing more than 20 strategies for you.

While all these methods of lead generation can be fantastically effective, they all have the potential for making you feel sleazy as well. Sleazy to yourself, and also sleazy to your customers.

Just imagine the following situations:

- someone on the sidewalk shoving a flyer in your hand, advertising a product you have zero interest in

- a window that pops up in the middle of the website you're viewing, totally interrupting what you're trying to do

- an ad in a magazine that makes some crazy, unbelievable claim - and after you read their stupid ad, you feel suckered for having "fallen for" the hook in the headline

Do YOU like it when businesses try to get your attention this way? Of course not. So you shouldn't employ these methods with your customers either. Unless you're okay with being sleazy, that is.

How can you avoid being sleazy in your lead generation?

The way you avoid sounding like a sleaze-ball in your lead gen is to always imagine that you're talking to your customer face to face. Live, and in person. If you feel no queasiness about delivering your message when you're looking your customer in the eye, then you know you're delivering a message that's authentic and heart-felt.

<u>The Recovering Sleaze-Ball Prescription for Lead Generation</u> If you happen to be a recovering sleaze-ball, and you're perfectly capable of looking a customer in the eye and dumping a load of crap on them to make the sale, then the prescription for you to begin your recovery is to ask yourself the following 3 questions:

1. Do you know for certain this person has the problem that you solve?
2. Are you truly offering a solution to that problem?

3. Is your solution better than any other one they could choose?

If your answer to any of those questions is no, then it's likely you're not serving the person by talking to them. You need to go back to the drawing board with either your Big Problem (Chapter 2), your Ideal Customer (Chapter 3), or both.

Also keep in mind that the purpose of lead generation is simply to find people to talk to about what you do - people who have the Big Problem you solve, that is.

Once you've found those people, now you can begin the process of awakening them more fully to their problem, demonstrating that you can solve that problem, and making it easy for them to pay you to do so. By now that process should be sounding familiar - it's our Sleaze-Free Sales Formula. And the next two chapters go into more detail about how to implement the rest of it.

In the remainder of this chapter, I've listed more than 20 different strategies for generating leads.   There are countless books and home study courses have been created to teach the nuances of all these strategies. It's way beyond the scope of this book to teach you, in detail, how to leverage each one of these strategies to generate new leads for your business.

What I have done instead is given you a brief overview of how each one of these strategies works, and some of the important facts you need to know.   Then I've listed resources you can turn to that will help you with whichever of the strategies you want to implement or improve in your business. Many of these resources are free; a few cost money.

What I encourage you to do is to review the complete list, and feel into which strategies appeal to you the most. Select 5 or 6 that you want to learn more about. Click those links and review the materials that are available.

Then choose 1, 2, or 3 strategies to commit to over the next 60 days. Don't choose more than 3 strategies, because you'll drown yourself and not implement anything. Also don't choose none - because without taking new action, you won't create new results!

There is additional help with your lead generation strategies at the end of this chapter, in the Action Plan.

Personal Networking

Many small business owners - especially those in the beginning phase of their business - rely heavily upon **personal networking** as a way of getting leads. And for many business owners, personal networking will always be the best way for them to get new customers.

Unfortunately, the vast majority of business owners are _lousy_ at networking! To succeed with personal networking, your mantra needs to be, "How can I help the other person?"

As we discussed in Chapter 4, you help them by getting to know them. Asking them questions. Then asking followup questions. Making sure your potential customer feels heard. A great technique for ensuring the other person feels heard is to simply re-state whatever they just said to you.

Unfortunately, most business owners are too self-involved to bother getting to know their prospects in this way. I once met a guy at a networking event who was a great example of doing this wrong.

This guy is in the printing business. And since he found out that I sell books and courses, he figured I would be a good customer for him. He assumed that I had the Big Problem he solves - the need for a good reliable printer. Based on his assumption, he immediately started pitching me on what he does - his price points, his customer service commitment, etc. Meanwhile, my eyes glazed over and I began to look for a way out of the conversation.

Because while it's true that I do in fact print books and courses all the time, I don't have the Big Problem he solves. Why? Because I've already got a good reliable printer. If you remember, "already having a guy" is one of the key variations of "I don't have a problem" we discussed in Chapter 4.

Does this mean he had no hope of doing business with me, or that it was a waste of time for both of us to talk to each other? Not at all. If he had taken a more skillful approach to the encounter, it might have turned out very differently.

If he had asked me questions and thereby impressed me with his salesmanship, I might have been open to hearing how great his service is. I might have recommended colleagues of mine to him - or heck I might have even given him a shot at a small portion of my own business.

In the next chapter, we're going to discuss how to approach a potential customer in a way that's not the slightest bit sleazy. The information contained in that chapter is useful for every lead generation strategy below; but it's the foundation of how to maximize your effectiveness with personal networking.

Word of Mouth

The second tactical approach to generating a lead is **word of mouth**. Word of mouth happens when somebody who has bought your product or service starts telling people about you, and encouraging them to come do business with you.

Word of Mouth Tactic #1: The Referral Program

Most of us that are in business get referrals every now and then. It's a by-product of being good at what you do - your customers like to tell their friends about you. However, having a structured referral program is a way of actively activating word of mouth marketing on your behalf.

The key components of a good referral program include:

- Thank them for being your customer
- Ask them to refer customers to you - and be specific as to what makes someone a good referral. In other words, share the characteristics of your Ideal Customer you developed earlier in this book.
- Give them a gift or special recognition when they refer customers to you.

How do you let customers know about your referral program? Here's a few ideas:

- Print a flyer or postcard, and drop it in every customer's bag at checkout
- Reserve a section of your online or print newsletter every month for your referral program
- Mention your referral program on your out-going telephone message
- Send an email to your customers. This is most effective when you're either kicking off your referral program, giving away the prize(s) for the winner(s) of your referral program, or giving recognition to someone for being a great referral source

And as with so many other marketing tactics, consistency is the key. Once you've launched your referral program, make sure and tell ALL your customers about it.

The following is an article that's loaded with great, practical advice about how to set up a referral program. Click to read it here: http://sleazefreeselling.com/ReferralProgram

Word of Mouth Tactic #2: Affiliate Marketing

Affiliate marketing is a tactic that's well-known in the online world. However, it's generally unknown to small business owners.

Affiliate marketing happens when two business owners get together and say, "I've got a group of buyers who listen to me when I make recommendations. You've got a really great product or service, that solves a problem my buyers have. How about I tell my buyers about your product or service, and you'll pay me a commission for everybody who buys?"

If it's a good match-up between the product and the buyers, then both business owners can win big-time with this strategy.

I was talking to somebody the other day who was doing a launch of her new home study course. She told me that 400 people registered for the teleseminar, on which she was going to be selling the course. Of those 400 registrants, 150 came from one affiliate.

So if it hadn't been for that one affiliate, the business owner with the home study course would have had a much smaller pool of potential customers on her call - so the arrangement was a win for her. And because the call did a good job of selling a high percentage of people into the home study course, the business owner who referred the 150 people got a nice healthy commission check - so the arrangement was a win for her too.

I'm utilizing affiliate marketing myself, right here in this chapter, by recommending specific products and services you might like to check out. While some of the resources I'm pointing you toward are free, most of them are provided by people or companies who would ultimately like to sell you something. And since I'm the one who introduced you to them, I can anticipate an affiliate commission when you begin to do business with them.

Just imagine if you were a business owner and I mentioned you in this book - don't you think you'd get an awful lot of leads from that? You sure would! (If you'd like me to mention you in one of my future books - or a revised edition of this book - please email Affiliates@SleazeFreeSelling.com)

To make affiliate marketing work for your business, think about what other business owners have groups of customers who might like to buy your product or service.

Decide how much you're willing to pay if that business owner sends customers your way. Then make it easy for that other business owner to say yes to you - write the sales copy, set up the shopping cart, be prepared with answers to all their potential questions.

Then it just becomes a matter of asking until somebody says yes!

Webinars are another great strategy for developing - and profiting from - affiliate marketing. Please see the section later in this chapter, "Automated Webinars," for more info.

There's also a fantastic peer group called Affiliate Marketers Group that offers training and puts on events, all geared how to be more effective and profitable with your affiliate marketing. To learn about their next networking and training event click here: http://sleazefreeselling.com/AMG

Word of Mouth Tactic #3: Social Media

By sharing what you are up to on social media, your friends and followers are naturally going to turn around and share your news with their friends. This is word of mouth marketing at its most organic.

This is easiest to do on Twitter, and it's called a retweet. If you say something interesting or helpful or funny or provocative, your followers can click one button and share that tweet of yours with all of their followers.

Sharing happens on Facebook in a couple ways. The most common is when somebody comments on something you've posted - a video or picture, for instance. They can also click the "share" button, if they really liked it, and post it to their own wall.

The best way to activate this social sharing aspect of social media is to engage in the conversation! Be social, comment on other people's tweets and posts, share their information with your audience. When you do this, pretty soon you'll discover that lots of people are also talking about YOU.

Social media also works well when you use it to specifically talk about the products and services you sell. But that counts as "Discovery Marketing," so I've gone into more detail about that use for social media further along in this chapter.

One of the best resources for all things social media is the Social Media Examiner website. Click here to learn more: http://sleazefreeselling.com/SocialMediaExaminer

Word of Mouth Tactic #4: Dumb Luck

Dumb luck is somebody just randomly sharing your marketing message. For example, one of your newsletter subscribers might think that a recent article was really good, and forward it to a friend of theirs, who in turn buys something from you that was mentioned elsewhere in the newsletter. You hadn't specifically asked your subscriber to do that (there was no "call to action" in the article); they just happened to like it and pass it on.

The same thing could happen if you create a flyer, or some sort of direct mail piece. The person you sent it to doesn't want it, but they end up either actually handing it so someone, and saying "Hey, I got this flyer, and I thought of you" or, they just leave it laying around. A few minutes later somebody walks by, sees it and thinks, "Oh wow, this looks really interesting," so they grab it and end up buying whatever the flyer was offering.

"Dumb Luck" obviously isn't something you can plan for. However, it's a common enough way for people to find out about you that I wanted to make sure you're aware of it.

Sharing What You Do With an Interested Audience

The third tactical approach to lead generation is **sharing what you do with an interested audience**. This method involves you speaking (in person, on video, over the airwaves ...) to a person or group of people who are already primed to hear you. They're waiting eagerly to hear what you have to say.

In this category of lead generation, you are actively putting out your message directly to customers. It's not word of mouth, because with word of mouth, you're depending upon somebody else to say, "This person's products and services are really good, and I think you should check them out."

Rather, in this second approach to lead generation, you're the one sharing what you do with an audience. You personally show up to talk about your own products and services.

Interested Audience Tactic #1: Speaking on Stage

Speaking on stage is just what it sounds like: someone gathers together an audience of people live in a room, and they invite you to stand at the front of the room with a microphone and talk.

Speaking on stage is arguably the best method known to man for establishing yourself as a credible authority figure. Someone else has invited you to speak, introduced you with a long list of all your accomplishments, and handed you a microphone. Now the audience sees you in the same light as the television news anchor, the lead singer of a rock band and their first grade teacher - all rolled into one.

Talk about power!

In other words, speaking onstage is a fantastic method for accomplishing Step 2 of our 3-Step Formula, "Demonstrate that you can solve their problem." If you're the undisputed expert, you're probably able to solve the problem, right?

I myself do a lot of seminar speaking. I also put on live events where I invite other speakers to address my audience. It's a great business model, whichever side of the equation you're on.

Lots of people teach courses, conduct live trainings and sell books that are about how to speak from the stage. Here are a few resources that I recommend:

James Malinchak - http://sleazefreeselling.com/JamesMalinchak
Lisa Sasevich - http://sleazefreeselling.com/LisaSasevich
Ali Brown - http://sleazefreeselling.com/AliBrown (Ali co-teaches this program with Lisa Sasevich)
Dan Kennedy - http://sleazefreeselling.com/DanKennedy

If you end up working with any of these people - tell them I sent you!

Interested Audience Tactic #2: Guest Blogging

In this day and age, there are ways to "gather an audience" that don't require people to physically gather in one spot. Blogs are a great example of this.

Whatever topic you specialize in, it's very likely that there exist numerous popular blogs that get a decent amount of traffic to them. And the owners of these blogs are always in need of fresh content. In fact, many blogs actively invite guest bloggers, and have a section of their website dedicated to that purpose. Just google "Become a Guest Blogger" and your area of expertise to start your search.

If you develop a relationship with the owner of that blog, they might let you write a guest post on their blog. And if it's a popular enough blog - and your article is well written enough - you could generate a healthy quantity of leads using this strategy.

Check out these articles for more:

14 Ways to Build Strategic Relationships with the Who's Who of Social Media
How to Get Invited to Be a Guest Blogger

Interested Audience Tactic #3: Being Interviewed

A close cousin of being a guest blogger is being interviewed. I've been interviewed many different times, in many different formats, on many different topics.

The kind of interview that might immediately pop to mind is radio interviews. What would it be like to be a guest on a top rated national radio program, like Sean Hannity, NPR's All Things Considered, Howard Stern or Tom Joyner?

And more importantly, what do you need to know to get considered by their producers? Most are looking for the same traits in their guests: surprising, weird and unconventional (what is your unique, compelling take on your subject of interest?) and 4-8 minute segments both in TV and radio, brevity and self editing is key.

You should always listen to audio of a show BEFORE you're a guest there to get a feel for the host's sense of humor, style and the rhythm and flow of conversation. Preparation is key!

And what's the best way to not only get invited back, but to parlay one radio interview into many more?   It's a simple...thank you. Thank you to the reporter who wrote about you; thank you to the radio host who had you on his or her show as a guest. Thank you to the cameraman from the TV station, who never gets any of the credit that gets gobbled up by the high profile anchor and reporter.

Remember, reporters and show hosts don't owe you anything; it's a privilege and honor that you've been given, and should be treated as such. The media is a very transient business, and saying thank you to media pros in one market will often help you in another market somewhere down the road. Plus, it's simply the right thing to do. To make your thank you really stand out, send a hand written note to the media pro.

To learn much more about the strategy of finding customers via radio publicity, I encourage you to check out my colleague Burke Allen at http://sleazefreeselling.com/BurkeAllen

Interested Audience Tactic #4: Telesummits

A telesummit is a gathering of experts, typically over a month-long period of time, who are all interviewed by the host. The experts share their particular take on whatever the theme of the telesummit is, and then they offer a product or service for those listeners who want to learn more.

Hosting a telesummit (or being a guest on one) is a fabulous way to impact thousands with your message, inspire lives and grow your business & income.

My friend Sage Lavine's Women on Purpose Speaker Series reached over 10,000 women from around the world and generated over 6 figures in sales, while Jeneth Blackert's New Wealth Experience has inspired tens of thousands to create true and lasting wealth and generated over $300,000 in sales.

If you're thinking to yourself, "Who am I to host a telesummit?" I encourage you to re-think that thought. The fact that you're interested in a book about "Sleaze-Free Selling" tells me you are exactly the person to create and host a life changing telesummit...especially if you're called to do it.

Make no mistake - lots of telesummits flop. But when you learn the right action, intention and structure, as well as how to position your telesummit so it stands out you can literally put your business on the map.

My friends Sage Lavine & Jeneth Blackert have made a name for themselves as some of the most successful telesummit hosts and trainers in the business. If you'd like to learn more from them, check out their training program. Click here for the training: http:// sleazefreeselling.com/telesummit

Interruption Marketing

The fourth tactical approach to lead generation is sharing what you do with people who don't necessarily want to hear about it, otherwise known as interruption marketing.

This category encompasses advertising of all kinds: radio advertising, television commercials, billboards on the side of the road, ads in the newspaper, flyers in the mail, Facebook ads, banner ads - all of it is interruption marketing.

Interruption marketing - or advertising - is highly dependent upon effective salesmanship. That makes sense, right? If you're going to "interrupt" your potential customer from what they're doing, and ask them to pay attention to what you're offering, you need to be very strong with every aspect of your offer.

It's also important that your message not only gets the person's attention, but that it succeeds at getting them to buy. After all, you're spending money on these ads - if you don't sell a lot of your products and services off of them, you'll very quickly be in the red.

It's because of these factors that Interruption Marketing has tended to spawn the sleaziest of lead generation tactics. You're basically walking up to someone who's in the middle of doing something, tapping them on the shoulder and saying, "Excuse me, I noticed you're fat. Would you like to try this magic diet pill?"

That said, interruption marketing is the most common - and, some would say, most effective - method for generating leads that exists today. So I can't write a book about salesmanship without including it.

And it is possible to do Interruption Marketing that's uplifting, rather than sleazy. So just try to stay on the "authentic" vs. the "sleazy" side of the line when crafting your advertising messages for your Interruption Marketing campaigns.

Interruption Marketing Tactic #1: PPC

"Pay per click," which is also known as PPC, is a very fast and efficient way to get a result with your marketing. You can actually have leads coming into your business within hours of setting up a campaign.

If you're looking into running a PPC campaign there are three primary sources to target, the best of those being Google AdWords, from a standpoint of possible prospect reach. Google is the most used search engine in the world. The second two would be Bing and Yahoo. Bing and Yahoo have now combined forces so you can actually create campaigns on both of those search engines through one portal.

A couple of considerations for running a PPC campaign include budgeting and your target market. You are going to have an expense outlay if you run a PPC campaign, however, you can limit it to the budget you choose. For instance you can set your campaign so it cannot exceed a spend of more than $10 per day, or whatever amount you choose.

Another consideration is your market. A highly competitive market like insurance can be very expensive, with a single click running as high as $30-$40. Some smaller markets like tanning salons may be very inexpensive, with each click as low as 30 to 40 cents. Imagine spending five dollars on ads and obtaining a $500 client. Not a bad return on investment.

My colleague Perry Marshall has written a very helpful e-course called "5 days to success with Google AdWords" and there's no charge for it. You can find out about it by clicking here: http://sleazefreeselling.com/PerryMarshall

Another colleague of mine, David Corbaley, offers a fantastic training program here: http://sleazefreeselling.com/PPC

Interruption Marketing Tactic #2: Facebook Ads

Buying traffic from Facebook is a radically different experience than Google AdWords and if you don't know these rules you're in for quite a surprise.

From *Ultimate Guide to Facebook Advertising* by Perry Marshall and Tom Meloche

Facebook offers extensive explanation within their site, about how to set up a Facebook ads campaign. It's not very difficult - you fill in a few blanks, decide how much you want to spend, upload a photo and you're off and running. The fact that it's easy doesn't guarantee it will be successful of course!

And one of the biggest criteria for whether or not your Facebook ads will be successful is whether you're using it to promote an appropriate kind of a business.

To find out if Facebook Ads is a good option for your business, I encourage you to take Perry Marshall's free assessment, "Is Facebook For Me?"

After answering a few simple questions about your business and your goals, you'll get a report of results from Perry about how effective - on a scale of 1 to 10 - you can expect Facebook Ads to be for your business.

I took the assessment myself, and found it to be very enlightening.

Interruption Marketing Tactic #3: Radio Advertising

Since radio has higher levels of target ability than most other direct response media, it offers businesses the ability to locate their Ideal Customers using specific demographics, geographics, and psychographics with precisely measured results.

Advertisers can therefore capitalize on the ability to target people from specific income brackets, age groups, religious affiliations, spending patterns, and more.

Much like with Pay Per Click, if you're gonna do radio advertising, you're well advised to hire an expert to guide your campaign. Because in order to develop an ad that works, you can expect to spend an easy five figures on advertising that _doesn't_ work, while you test and tweak the process.

The ideal formula for a radio commercial includes utilizing a Trust Agent or spokesperson (like William Shatner for Priceline.com), a perceived problem with a solution, testimonials to reinforce the solution, a free offer or offers, and a call to action.

Not very different than the formula I've been teaching you throughout this book, is it?

Radio advertising is also a lot less expensive than you might think, especially when you work with somebody who knows what they're doing to buy the ads for you. A seasoned expert can typically pick up a whole bunch of extra advertising slots for free, along with the ones you paid for. And without that person in your corner, your advertising message would get a lot less exposure.

Someone I know personally and highly recommend is Fred Catano of Bullerdozer Digital. Click here to learn more about what Fred & radio advertising can do for your business: http://sleazefreeselling.com/FredCatano

Interruption Marketing Tactic #4: Direct Mail

Direct mail is one of the most effective ways to build your business, increase your client base, and make loads of cash in the process. But only when you incorporate the Sleaze-Free Sales Formula into your mailing pieces!

In a recent study of 18-34 year old females at Ball State University, it was determined that **72%** of them wanted to receive their marketing messages via Direct Mail while only **53%** of them wanted to receive them via email.

And none of them, **0%** wanted to receive marketing messages via their phone or by text message. They simply considered it intrusive, ie, sleazy.

In order to succeed with Direct Mail as a lead generation strategy, the most important thing to do is to treat your mailing piece as an Initial Offer - one that addresses your customer's Big Problem and leads them to your Big Offer.

The next chapter, Chapter 6, explains in detail exactly what an Initial Offer is, and how to craft your Initial Offer so that it most effectively generates sales for you.

When you do this in your Direct Mail, your client or prospect will be compelled to get up and do something right then and there, in that very moment. If they don't, you've most likely lost them

Strategy Check:

The Big Problem that you came up with in Chapter 2 should work as the headline on a postcard or flyer.

The Corcoran's Big Problem is a great example: "Is Your Upstairs Bedroom Always Too Hot, No Matter How High You Crank The A/C?"

Tweak your Big Problem if you need to, in order to make it headline-worthy!

forever. Your mailing piece will go in the can, along with the rest of the day's discarded "junk" mail.

Business owners who say, "I tried Direct Mail and it didn't work for me" are usually guilty of sending "Me Too" advertising, as opposed to treating their mailing piece as an Initial Offer.

"Me Too" advertising is when your ad or message looks the same as everyone else's in your industry. It features your hours and location, as well as your logo right at the top, nice and big, taking up the most important "real estate" on the page.

The worst part of "Me Too" advertising is that it's boring. It looks like every other ad your customer gets in their mailbox, so it gets thrown straight into the trash can, along with the rest of the "junk mail". Why would you expect them to do anything else?

On the other hand, if you stand out - if you do something even a little different than what your potential customers are used to seeing - you will have done more to capture their attention than pretty much anybody else they get mail from every day.

Direct Mail does not have to be expensive. There are a variety of ways to do Direct Mail that will get great results without you feeling as if you have mortgaged your business to do it. Here are a few inexpensive ways to get started in direct mail:

• Simple Postcards
• Self-Mailers (anything not requiring an envelope, like a fold-over flyer)
• A sales letter and order form in a standard envelope

The best way to keep your costs down on Direct Mail, however, is to learn from an expert how to do it right! My colleague, Diane Conklin, is widely respected as one of the top Direct Mail experts in the industry. She's been running successful Direct Mail campaigns for years, and she teaches you the nuts and bolts in her course, "Direct Mail Made Easy."

Learn more and get a copy of her free CD here: http://sleazefreeselling.com/DirectMailMadeEasy

Discovery Marketing

The fifth and final method of generating a lead has positively exploded with the advent of social media these last few years, and it's been dubbed **Discovery marketing.** Discovery marketing is what's happening when a consumer has a problem, so they go looking for a solution - typically online.

But rather than going directly to someone selling a product like we did in the old days (via the Yellow Pages, for instance), they go on a quest for information. And what they find is blog posts, articles, videos, podcasts, social media posts ... in short, they find millions and millions of bits of web-hosted information that addresses their problem.

Savvy business owners have discovered that these bits of information can be powerful methods of enticing new customers into the fold. And that's why we see a staggering amount of new information being generated every day.

This section details some of the most common methods for business owners to generate bits of information like this, in order to make themselves most discoverable by potential customers who are looking for solutions to their problems this way.

Discovery Marketing Tactic #1: Be An Author

This first Discovery Marketing tactic may look, at first glance, like it doesn't belong in this category. But remember what's at the heart of this tactic - your customer has a problem, and they are searching on their own for a solution to it. As long as people are still turning to books and bookstores for solutions to their problems, your customers can find you with this tactic.

Additionally, being an author is one of the most time-tested strategies for becoming known as an expert in your field:

- Whenever a magazine article quotes somebody as an expert, they follow with their credentials. Most often those credentials are either a fancy degree, or the fact that they're the author of a book.
- The widely-accepted phrase, "I wrote the back on that subject," means, "I'm an expert."
- Books have been associated with knowledge and wisdom for centuries. It's hard-wired into our school-children brains to trust whatever we read in print, and to respect the authority of whoever wrote it.

To fully grasp the power of being an author, imagine this scenario. You're at a cocktail party, and some self-proclaimed expert is spouting off their theories on some new, controversial or complex subject. How likely are you to stop and engage with them, to hear what they have to say? Not very. You might even dismiss them as a quack.

But if that very same person were to espouse those very same theories between the pages of a published book, you - and a whole lot of others - might give careful consideration to what he was saying.

Now imagine that you're the one who's espousing theories, within the pages of your very own book. And let's further imagine that along with those theories which you espouse, your book also incorporates the 3 steps of the Sleaze-Free Sales Formula.

When all that is true, your book now becomes an extremely effective Initial Offer. (For more details about using an Initial Offer as an effective business-building tool, continue reading in Chapter 6).

But how do you get your book published?

Traditional publishing

Getting your book published by a traditional publisher isn't the easiest thing to do. In fact, the difficulty of getting a publisher to notice you is exactly what has kept so many would-be authors from realizing their dream.

My colleague David Hancock recognized this problem some time ago, and set out to fix it. He is the author of "Guerrilla Marketing for Writers," and is also the founder of Morgan James Publishing, a traditional publishing house that takes a very non-traditional approach to publishing its authors.

Morgan James has trademarked the phrase "The Entrepreneurial Publisher™" because of their unique collaboration approach with authors and other publishers, treating them as partners rather than solely as intellectual property suppliers.

Well known traditionally published authors including Jay Conrad Levinson (*Guerrilla Marketing*), Brendon Burchard (*The Millionaire Messenger*), and Joe Vitale (*The Attractor Factor*), have chosen to publish titles with

Morgan James because of the company's innovative way of doing business.

To learn more about Morgan James Publishing and its various imprints - and to submit a work to be published - visit http://sleazefreeselling.com/GuerillaMarketingforWriters

According to David and Morgan James Publishing, here are the Guerrilla Author's Marketing 10 Commandments:

1. Create books, products, and services that you can market with pride and passion.
2. Remember that you are in the service of your ideas, your books, and your readers.
3. Establish an annual marketing budget that reflects your belief in the importance of marketing and enables you to carry out your promotion plan.
4. Devote the same time, energy, and imagination to promoting your books every day that you devoted to writing them.
5. Foster and sustain warm, giving relationships with your networks.
6. Maintain the perspective of a one-person multimedia, multinational conglomerate when you make decisions about writing and promoting your books.
7. Be a lifelong learner in your field and in learning to market your business so you remain competitive.
8. Use state-of-the-art techniques and technology to serve your readers better.
9. Recommend competitors' books if they will meet readers' needs in ways that yours don't.
10. Practice "co-opetition" by seeking ways to benefit from collaborating with your competitors.

Self-Publishing

If self-publishing is more your style, that route is rapidly becoming easier, more profitable and more respected - thanks in large part to Amazon Kindle.

Here's 5 facts you probably didn't know about the Kindle:

Fact #1: You don't need an actual Kindle. You don't need a Kindle to read Kindle books (or write or publish them) - there's a Kindle app you can download for your smartphone, Mac or PC.

Fact #2: Easy Updates. Your Kindle books can be updated in an instant, and as often as you want. Find a typo? No problem! Want to update a fact in your book? Do it in seconds, rather than waiting for the next edition of your book to come out.

Fact #3: Customers love buying from Amazon! Amazon is the friendly, familiar mega-store that so many of us are used to shopping on. We trust Amazon - and by extension, we trust everybody who sells on Amazon. Many people don't even realize there are sellers on Amazon totally un-related to Amazon itself.

Plus, Amazon has over 200,000,000 credit cards on file - this means that 200 million consumers have a _very_ low barrier to buying your book.

Fact #4: Earn decent royalties. You can actually make a decent living selling books! You've probably heard the conventional wisdom, "You're never gonna make any money off your book - you just want to have it as a positioning tool." With traditional publishing, that was certainly true for most authors. But when you self-publish on the Kindle, you can earn as much as $7.46 for every book you sell. Sell 100 books a month, and you've got a car payment - maybe even rent.

Fact #5: Readers LOVE Kindle. The popular Hunger Games series sold 4 times as many copies on Kindle as it did in print.

How do you turn a Kindle book into leads for your business?

With a traditional book, there's a fairly indirect route between someone buying your book (your Initial Offer) and them buying your Big Offer. Sure, the reader might love what you have to say so much that they seek you out online and end up becoming a customer. If you have a very marketing-savvy publisher, that publisher might let you put a page in the back of the book that describes your Big Offer, and encourages people to buy it from you. But with either of these methods, the percentage of readers who end up buying your Big Offer is quite small.

With Kindle, it's a whole new ball game.

For starters, Amazon wants to sell your books as much as you do - so they help you a whole lot. Have you ever noticed the recommendations Amazon gives you as a buyer? They serve up those recommendations via the "Recommended For You" section, as well as the "Customers Also Viewed" section.

When you have multiple books listed on Amazon, anybody who buys one book will immediately be offered another of your books. If you only have one book, Amazon will still recommend it to readers who buy works from other authors - assuming your book is highly ranked on Amazon.

Another reason that publishing on Kindle is a great strategy for you as a business owner is that you can build your list with people who buy your Kindle book. How? By offering some kind of a freebie within the pages of your book. When readers click on it (remember, a Kindle book is essentially a website), they're taken to a page on your website where they can opt in for your free thing.

For an example of how this works, you can see my "free thing" here: http://sleazefreeselling.com/ FREEAudiobook It's a free copy of the audiobook version of this book. While you're there, get yourself a copy!

Publishing on Kindle is my own personal favorite strategy of the moment, and I've developed a short, information-packed training about how to leverage Kindle publishing to grow your business. You can find out more about my training here: http://sleazefreeselling.com/ KindleTraining

Discovery Marketing Tactic #2: Twitter

Twitter is a vital component in the social media machine. Those who choose to ignore it because they don't "get" it are missing out on a major asset for their business. If you doubt there could be any power in 140-character micro-blogging, consider that Twitter is consistently ranked by Alexa as the 8th or 9th most-trafficked site on the globe.

On top of this, we need to take into account the fact that the vast majority of regular Twitter users today manage their Twitter accounts using third-party apps such as Hootsuite, TweetDeck or Social Oomph. This means the amount of time spent on the actual Twitter site itself is a mere fraction of the time actually spent by people using Twitter remotely.

What all of this means is that Twitter is a powerful platform for Discovery Marketing.

Millions of people a day are looking at tweets. And they're not just looking at tweets in their Twitterstream. Because Twitter is considered by Google to be a "high-authority site," Google returns tweets very high in its search engine results. So if you're active on Twitter, it's very likely that when someone Googles your name, your product or company, or even the category of service that you provide - your Tweets will show up on page one of Google!

It's vital that you really nail your Twitter foundations: constructing an effective, clear Twitter profile; learning to write a really compelling Tweet; and what it takes to attract the right kinds of followers.

Once you've mastered the basics of Twitter, now how do we develop a marketing campaign that will be effective on Twitter? One that speaks differently to the different types of people in your Twitter following? And most important of all, how do you build relationships on Twitter that take into account the dynamic nature of that platform, and which offer different degrees of closeness to the people within your Twitterverse.

Answering these questions - and trying to keep up with the answers, as the platform keeps changing - can be overwhelming or off-putting to many business owners. I was one of them, frankly - until I read a fabulous new book called Tweep-e-licious, by Lynn Serafinn. She answers all these questions I've just posed and more - I couldn't recommend her book more highly. Click here to buy Tweep-e-Licious now on Amazon: http://sleazefreeselling.com/Tweep-e-Licious

Discovery Marketing Tactic #3: Online Video

Did you know ... 85% of your customers are more likely to buy your product or service if they have watched a video about it first.   By 2013, it's estimated that 90% of all internet traffic will be video-based.

But the best part is that for many highly competitive keywords, you'll often see a very small business ranked in the top 5, or even top 3, positions on Google - when that ranking is a video listing.

Why is that?

Because even though "everybody knows" that video is one of the best ways to get found on the internet, and to consequently get traffic to your website, Fan Page or even your brick and mortar store ... so many businesses still skip video as a part of their marketing strategy! The lesson is that if you would just DO videos (and then properly promote them), you would get results. Plain and simple.

Promoting videos

I'll admit that I'm guilty of under-utilizing video to an embarrassing extent. I have several dozen videos on my YouTube channel, most of which I never did anything to promote. Consequently, my views are only in the double- and triple digits for most of my videos.

But I have a handful of videos that all have between 4,000 and 6,000 views - and one video that, as of this publishing, has over 25,000 views. What did I do to get those views? I hired these guys: http://sleazefreeselling.com/VideoBlueprint

I highly recommend you check out their Video Blueprint, if you're serious about using video to market your products and services.

<u>Creating Superstar Quality Business Videos</u>

Videos that compel and engage an audience are magical. Really.

Who can forget that famous Google video, "Parisian Love?" (see the screenshot below) In 52 seconds of Google searches set to music, that video took us on an emotional journey rarely achieved by a commercial. And - as many would-be copycats learned - it's a whole lot harder than it might look to create that kind of magic.

That's why I'm so excited about Films About Me, a process created by Emmy Award® winning Director David Gumpel & Social Media Marketing Expert Catherine Hedden. Their process produces business marketing videos that capture your customer's attention from the start and keep them engaged though the entire video.

They have a magic formula that uncovers your passions, your vision, your hopes and dreams, and bottles that into a film your customers can hear, see and feel.

Even though their formula is magic, it is based in solid research in great storytelling, proven sales and marketing strategies and award-winning film-making.

They start with fully understanding your brand and the emotional connection you have to your clients. Then they capture your passion and vision during filming. And finally, they use their magic formula to edit your Film About Me so that it engages your clients and moves them to action.

To learn more about David and Catherine's magic Films About Me process, visit http://sleazefreeselling.com/FilmsAboutMe

Discovery Marketing Tactic #4: Article Marketing

The biggest misconception a lot of business owners have is that article marketing is an SEO tactic, not a means of generating traffic. You're not using articles for backlinks with the anchor text of your choosing, but rather, you're generating content which drives qualified leads to your site.

Whether you have more time than money, or money than time, you need to get these articles written. You can do so by writing the articles yourself (excess of time) or by hiring someone to write them for you (excess of money).

There are 7 pitfalls to avoid with article marketing:
1. Quality over quantity - going for quality ALONE
2. Too much hype / bragging
3. Making your content too broad (avoid the head of the long tail)
4. Failure to deliver on the article title within article body. If your title says "10 things ..." you need to actually list 10 things in the article.
5. Trusting ghostwriters - this is a Big Problem, or it can be. It's one of the biggest ways that your articles could start to suck.
6. Submission infrequency - it's much better to publish one article once a week than 2 today, 5 a week from now, none for a month ...
7. Failure to create scalable systems. With article marketing, quantity is important. If you're going to dive into it, you want to have systems in place that allow you to churn out a lot of articles.

One final tip - the bio and resource box is the most important part of your article. In it, you want to include the words, "Click here for your FREE ..." because the words "click here" and "free" generate more clicks than anything else.

EzineArticles.com is far and away the most important site on which to syndicate your articles. And they offer an extensive library of training articles that cover all the most important information about how to succeed with article marketing. Check out this great free resource by clicking here: http://sleazefreeselling.com/EzineArticles

Discovery Marketing Tactic #5: Google Plus Local

As of the publication of this book, Google seems to be going more local with their search results. This is obvious from the standpoint of a searcher. If you do a search on a given topic or market you'll see that Google serves up many local results on the first page.

These results include Google maps, which is currently called Google Plus Local (previously it was called Google places). You can recognize this by the little pushpins next to the listings, and they correspond to the letter on the map to the right of the search. For example if you're looking at the search result that has an "A" in the pushpin you can look on the map and see that same "A" and the location of the business.

Google plus local is one of the best positions to have your business ranked. If you can rank in the top one or two positions of Google plus local and have the other components that make a successful listing as well, such as 10+ reviews and a high review score, you WILL get more business.

Setting up your Google plus local account should be one of your top priorities when first setting up an online marketing campaign for your business. You'll need to confirm your account and Google will send you a postcard with a verification PIN. This can take up to three weeks to receive, so set up your initial account and then go onto other things such as PPC and SEO while you wait for your verification. Once you verify your account with the PIN that Google sends you, you're then able to go in and optimize your Google plus local account for best results.

Click here to learn more about using Google Plus Local effectively in your business: http://sleazefreeselling.com/GooglePlusLocal

Discovery Marketing Tactic #6: SEO

Search engine optimization, also known as SEO, is one of the best ways to get a lot of traffic to your business's website. When done correctly SEO can be one of the most powerful forms of online marketing, and very cost effective as well.

Note: there are those who now claim it can be very difficult to get reliable organic SEO for a lot of business categories. But since it's still a strategy many experts swear by, I've included it here.

With SEO, you do what's called "optimizing your website," or webpages within your site, targeting a specific keyword or small group of keywords. This is how the search engines know what that specific webpage or website is about. When somebody does a search about that topic, if your SEO is done correctly, Google will serve up your listing as one of the top-ranked websites.

"On page optimization" is the actual optimization of the website and webpages themselves, which can be very detailed. The other component is "offsite optimization" which includes other websites linking back to your website.

A primary consideration when setting up an SEO campaign is the time is going to take. Many people under estimate the value of SEO but they also underestimate the time involved and the time that it takes to get the benefit of doing SEO for your business. Depending on the competition and your market it can take months to get your site ranked on the first page.

If you have a good SEO company that it knows what they're doing you can become a dominant force in your market and rank very high, and you can do it rather quickly. The top three spots are the best to have from SEO standpoint. You may hear SEO companies state things like "we can get you on page 1 of Google" which isn't that big of a deal. If you're on page one but down at the bottom at number nine, only about 2% of your prospects are going to see you anyway. You need to shoot for the top position and not be satisfied until you get there.

A good SEO company is hard to find, but my friend David Corbaley is worth checking out: http://sleazefreeselling.com/SEO

Discovery Marketing Tactic #7: Press Releases

Many business owners mistakenly think of the press release as a marketing dinosaur - right up there with fax machines and typewriters. The truth is, however, that press releases are one of the strongest methods for generating leads online that exist today.

By publishing news announcements about your company and products, you receive continuous exposure to your target audience. And, because your press releases include links to your website, your site will rank higher in the search engines for your most important keywords.

A few important elements of successful press release marketing include:

- Commit to publishing at least once a week. Once you get over feeling like your "news" has to be earth-shattering, this will get a lot easier.
- Distribute your press release. Some of the top choices for press release distribution are Online PR News, PRWeb and SubmitPressRelease 123.
- Stockpile your press releases on your website.
- Leverage your press releases by making sure to include your social sharing links on every press release.
- Stack your press releases - include a link to your previously published press releases in your newest press releases for an exponential effect.

Here's an online tool I discovered that automatically generates and formats press releases for you, after you input your data: http://sleazefreeselling.com/InstantPressReleaseTool

But generating a properly formatted press release is only the first step. There is a magic to getting results from your press releases - and a few years ago I was fortunate enough to stumble across a true magician. His name is Mark Maupin, and I was positively floored by the results I got for my real estate business after hiring Mark to do a round of press releases for me.

Not only did my press releases show up at the top of the Google search results for several of my keywords, they _stayed there_ ... for YEARS. And I know a number of other savvy marketers who have used Mark and gotten similarly impressive results from his work.

To talk to Mark about helping you jump start your press release marketing, get hold of him here: http://

<u>sleazefreeselling.com/MarkMaupin</u> And tell him I said hi!

Discovery Marketing Tactic #8: White Papers

If you sell any kind of complex service, technology or sophisticated product, a White Paper is the best way to educate your customers about that technology.

You can use a white paper to build your credibility, get free exposure in the press, attract new customers, and drive new technology into change-resistant, conservative markets.

Most white papers are either too technical (boring) or too commercial (thin and cheesy. But what's most important of all, though, is promoting and publicizing your white paper - because the best white paper in the world is no good unless somebody reads it!

Perry Marshall wrote the Definitive Guide to Writing and Promoting White Papers, and you can get it for free here: <u>http://sleazefreeselling.com/WhitePapers</u>

Add-On Tools & Resources

CopyDoodles

No matter what kind of lead generation strategy you use, there's almost always an element of text-based marketing, or copywriting. And whenever we're talking about copywriting, we're always looking for nuances - small tweaks that can increase your readership and increase your conversion rates.

A number of famous copywriters have commented on handwriting being an effective technique in copy design.

Drayton Bird said, "The use of handwritten notes in the margins can add variety and interest to the eye and brain." Ted Nicholas noted, "A good way to gain more attention for important blocks of copy is by using handwritten notes in the margins." And David Olgivy has also emphasized the same.

Back in the "old days," copywriters would literally hand write portions of their ads, like in the ad below for Modern Mechanix from 1938.

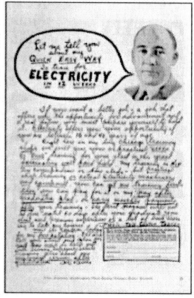

But with the technology available today, writing by hand in your copy is no longer necessary. While there are lots of sources for handwriting fonts, the go-to resource for every marketer and small business owner I know is CopyDoodles, a power-house copywriting enhancement tool created by Mike Capuzzi.

In our crazy world of constantly being bombarded with media and advertisements, CopyDoodles creates the feeling of personalization on all your marketing pieces, making your readers feel important, special, and as though you are connecting to them on a one-on-one basis.

Thousands of business owners and entrepreneurs in over 35 countries around the world use CopyDoodles online and offline to improve their marketing.

Whether you work from home or the local coffee shop, own a brick and mortar store, see patients on an hourly basis, or work in a corporate office in Manhattan, CopyDoodles can improve your marketing as it already has for many businesses.

CopyDoodles can be used to enhance a sales letter, a web page or even a direct mail piece. Below is a very simple example of what can be done with CopyDoodles:

Before
CopyDoodles

After
CopyDoodles

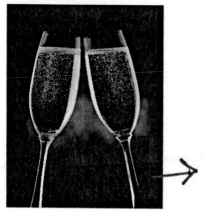

Like with most marketing techniques, there is a strategy to effectively using CopyDoodles. You have to know when you use it, where you use, and why you use it. Here are a few tips for using CopyDoodles effectively:

- Emphasize important points in your copy with a CopyDoodle
- Keep it real & authentic
- Stick to one color of CopyDoodles throughout any given piece
- Also use just one font
- Watch how you resize - you want your CopyDoodle big enough to be eye-catching, but not so big that it overtakes the rest of your message
- Watch your print quality - the effectiveness of your CopyDoodle will be blown if it's all pixelated

- Rotate CopyDoodles to give them that "I just wrote this for you" look and feel
- Flip CopyDoodles to quickly add a mirror effect
- Stretch CopyDoodles to easily change their appearance and to make them fit

To learn more about how CopyDoodles can enhance all of your copywriting materials, get Mike Capuzzi's ebook, "3 Steps to Incredible Response" by clicking here: http://sleazefreeselling.com/CopyDoodles

Automated Webinars

I put webinars into this final, catch-all category because they can be used in a number of different ways, each of which fall into a different lead generation category.

Webinars are great ways to build your subscriber list via joint ventures (JVs). Ask others to promote your webinar in exchange for a share of the profits from any sales done through your event. Not only will you have a great webinar, but you will build your list at the same time! (Check out the section of this chapter called Affiliate Marketing for more info).

Another great way to implement automated webinars is to conduct expert interviews. Locate the best people in your field, and allow them to share their expertise with your audience. This is a particularly good strategy if you yourself aren't yet an expert in your field (or you don't think you are).

Using either of the models above, many people have turned their best webinars into stand alone products like audio recordings, written transcripts, and home study products. You are only limited by your imagination.

Now that we have established some rationale for webinars, how does one go about getting it done? It's simple; just follow these steps:

- Choose a compelling topic.
- Prepare a modest outline of what your webinar should look like.
- Solicit advice from affiliates, JV partners etc. about what products to
  offer for sale during the webinar.
- Produce promotional material.
- Create and upload an opt-in registration page to capture each
  participant's contact information.
- Coordinate the webinar promotion with the JV partners and/or
  colleagues.
- Remind sign-ups about the webinar (i.e. Call-in details; expert
  biography, etc.)
- It's show time! Perform your webinar hosting duties, or bring in the
  professional interviewer.

For the uninitiated, webinars may seem like an "advanced" marketing tactic that requires deep technical knowledge.

Nothing could be further than the truth! Thanks to advances in webinar and web simulcasting software, running your own webinar/ teleseminar can be simple as pressing a few buttons!

Learn how you can Maximize Your Webinars Success with this free training: "How to Create Recurring Webinars and Teleseminars" http://sleazefreeselling.com/AutomatedWebinars

~~~~~~

Action Plan - Where do you get most of your leads?

Go through your list of 25 customers from Chapter 3. Where did those customers come from (which lead generation strategy did you use to acquire them)? Based upon that information, make a list of the top 5 lead generation strategies that currently work for you:

_____

_____

_____

What lead generation strategies could you add to the mix? Based upon the overview I've provided in this chapter, what strategies do you feel drawn to? If you're not currently knowledgeable about those strategies, commit to learning about them!

_____

_____

Important: pick no more than THREE new strategies. Learn about them. Then _implement_ them. It's a colossal waste of time and money to continually chase shiny objects without ever taking any actual action.

~~~~~~

For help with lead generation strategies, visit

http://juliakline.com/members/ask-a-question/

Submit a question and get an answer from me, personally, within 24 hours!

This is a limited time offer, to promote this book. Eventually the page - and the chance to ask questions - will no longer be available free of charge. So go there now!

~~~~~~

If you're having a hard time deciding which lead generation strategies appeal to you most, part of your problem may be that you don't know what you're going to say to people when they stop to listen to you.

That's what the next chapter is all about - how to approach your customers in such a way that they first stop and listen, and then they ask you to tell them more.

... CONTINUE TO THE NEXT CHAPTER ...

Chapter 6: How to talk to a potential customer about buying, without feeling like a sleaze-ball

The previous chapter was a sampler platter of more than 20 different marketing strategies you could utilize in order to reach customers - ie, to generate leads.

Now that you've got people to talk to, you need to start talking to them! And not just "cheap cocktail conversation," as my old Sales Manager, Ted Sveda, always used to say. You want to have conversations that lead directly to a discussion about buying from you. In marketing lingo, you want to use sales conversations as a way to make an offer.

"Making an offer" is the part of the sales process that business owners often feel is the most sleazy. It's the part where you talk about what you do, state your price and put out your hand for the check.

Re-read that last sentence. Does it make you feel a little nauseous? Or like you want to give up on this Sleaze-Free Sales Formula right now? Good. The first step to increased wealth is becoming conscious of your own discomfort zone. Now keep reading ...

The fact is, there is nothing sleazy about being paid for what you do.

I repeat: there is nothing sleazy about being paid for what you do!

You might be the kind of business owner who finds it easy to approach a potential customer and start talking to them - maybe even about their problems and how you could solve them. But then you don't know how to turn that friendly chat with an interested prospect into a discussion of how that prospect could pay you for your products and services.

If this is you, you're not willing to be paid for what you do. What will happen to you, if you don't fix this problem, is that you will go out of business.

So let's figure out how to fix this problem without being sleazy, shall we?

Sleazy vs. Non-Sleazy

We've established there's nothing sleazy about being paid for what you do. There is also nothing sleazy about _asking_ to be paid for what you do.

But if you start every conversation with every person you encounter by saying, "Here's what I do and here's how you pay me to do it," you're being sleazy. Or if not sleazy, you're at least being obnoxious, pushy and rude.

You'll soon discover that not only will this approach make customers run the other way whenever they see you coming, it's not even particularly effective.

By starting every single conversation with your pushy sales pitch, what you're doing wrong is you're not bothering to ask questions and find out whether or not the person you're talking to has the Big Problem that you solve. Neither are you investigating to see whether they meet the other criteria you established in Chapter 3 that would make them your Ideal Customer. And finally, your offer itself probably lacks elegance. It's not easy to say yes to.

Note: While the previous scenario most often plays out when you meet with a potential customer in person, the same basic psychology can happen online or in print advertising too.

One Way to Do It Right

The trick to making an offer with elegance, and not a whiff of sleaze, is to know how to ask, who to ask, and when to ask. The best way I've found to get this right every time is to develop a 2-step offer:

> Step 1: Your Initial Offer. Your Initial Offer should be something low-cost or even free that makes it easy for a potential customer to say "yes" to continuing the conversation with you.

> Step 2: Your Big Offer. Your Big Offer is the main product or service. It's the thing you were trying to sell in the first place.

The second step - your Big Offer - should be familiar to you. It's the part of the sales conversation you've been doing all along.

The first step, however, may be a new concept to you. It's what I call your Initial Offer.

Utilizing an Initial Offer allows you to approach your

customer elegantly, and without a whiff of sleaze, because you're basically just offering them a free taste. And if it's a taste of something that addresses their Big Problem (which it must, as I explain later in this chapter), who wouldn't be happy to accept that?

Your Initial Offer also requires them to give you their name, email, phone number, or address. Some marketers would tell you that the whole point of the Initial Offer is to acquire this contact information, so that you can follow up with them later (more about this in Chapter 7).

But I believe the best part of your Initial Offer is that when you craft it carefully, it   can turn the conversation, just as elegantly as it was begun, to a discussion of your Big Offer - and in so doing, generates sales for you!

That's right - when you put thought and care into your Initial Offer, it actually can make the sale of your Big Offer for you:

- If your Initial Offer is a free consultation - a meeting with the customer in person or on the phone - you can often close them on your Big Offer during this live meeting. The "script" that you follow during this free consultation should set you up for this.

- If your Initial Offer is some kind of packaged information - a free report, a DVD, a pamphlet or brochure - it should always include an order form. If the report, DVD, pamphlet or brochure does a good job of answering all their questions, they will often go ahead and send in the order form for your Big Offer on the spot.

- If your Initial Offer is a well-designed group training of some kind - a webinar, an evening workshop, a tele-class - many of them will to say yes to your Big Offer at the end of the training.

How to Craft Your Initial Offer

Later in this chapter I present a number of case studies of good Initial Offers. By reading them you'll get ideas for what your own Initial Offer could be. But here are the basic components you want to consider.

1. Your Initial Offer should always be something that sets you up to present your Big Offer, or the main thing you sell. So before developing your Initial Offer, think about what your Big Offer is. Hold that thought in mind as you create your Initial Offer.

129

2. Your Initial Offer must address your customer's Big Problem - because that's what's going to make them stop what they're doing and listen to you. There's something they're worrying about, lying awake at night thinking about, searching for a solution to. When you name it, and offer to solve it, they'll pay attention.

3. Of course your Initial Offer can't solve the customer's Big Problem completely - then they wouldn't need your Big Offer! But it should _address_ their Big Problem. Continue reading to the case studies later in this chapter for examples of what I'm talking about.

4. Another key element of your Initial Offer is that it must give you a chance to shine. It should let you do the thing you're absolutely best at doing - and thereby demonstrate that you would be great at solving their Big Problem once and for all, after they hire you to do so by buying your Big Offer.

5. And that brings us back around to where we started. Your Initial Offer must include within it a discussion of your Big Offer, as an integrated, natural out-growth of the Initial Offer itself. The transition from

> *"Let me offer you some free help as a part of this Initial Offer,"*

to

> *"My Big Offer will help you so much more than this Initial Offer can; let me tell you about it and how you can get started today."*

must be smooth and elegant. Both you and your customer should feel comfortable making the transition.

As an aside, your Initial Offer must also perform one important logistical function. It must capture their contact information! Whether your Initial Offer is a free report online, a free (or paid) consultation over the phone or in person, or a brochure you'll send through the mail - your customer must give you their name and contact information in order to receive it. This is so that you can follow up with them. Because as we'll see in Chapter 7, followup marketing is an essential element in the success of the Sleaze-Free Sales Formula.

The 2-Step Offer In Practice

Let's imagine that you're a mortgage broker, and your Big Offer is a home loan. You've determined that your customer's Big Problem is that while they want to buy a house, they don't know if they can qualify for a mortgage or not - they're totally confused by the state of the housing and credit industries today.

You need an Initial Offer which will attract home-loan seekers, by offering to clear up their confusion for them.

How do you do that?

The answer depends on which lead generation strategy you're going to use to approach people.

If you're generating leads online, a terrific Initial Offer is a free report. As a mortgage broker, you could develop a 10-pg free report about the three surprising facts about home loans in America in late 2012. There is so much misinformation right now about what is and what is not possible with home loans today, a free report like that would be an enticing way to get your Ideal Customer interested in talking to you.

That Free Report then becomes your Initial Offer. You host it on a web page somewhere, or even on your blog, and when potential customers come to that page, they give you their name and email address, and you send them the Free Report. The Free Report itself includes a description of your services as a loan officer, and asks them to take action - call you, make an appointment online, etc.

(For those potential customers who don't take action on your Big Offer immediately after reading your Free Report, you need to implement a followup marketing campaign. The next chapter, Chapter 7, will discuss how to do that).

If you're generating leads in person however, you wouldn't want to offer a Free Report - that would be a little awkward, wouldn't it? Standing at a networking event with a drink in one hand and a stack of Free Reports in the other?

So for that lead generation strategy, you need to come up with a different Initial Offer. A very common Initial Offer after meeting at a networking event is a followup conversation, either on the phone or in person. To entice the maximum number of potential customers to take you up on this Initial Offer - to agree to meet with you later - you might say that in that conversation, you will explain the Three Surprising Facts About Home Loans in America - which is the same content as you put in your Free Report online.

When you offer to have this conversation, the person might say to you, "Well what are the three facts? Can't you just tell me right now?"

So you need to be prepared to share with them one fact on the spot - something that will genuinely be helpful, and also pique their interest in learning more from you.

But then to cement the Initial Offer, you can say something like, "The other two facts take more than 30 seconds to explain, so I can't go into them right here, with a cocktail in our hands. Plus if we're sitting at my desk when we talk, then I can run a preliminary credit report for you, and give you some concrete facts as opposed to just conjecture."

Do you see what I did there? I gave them a reason to accept my Initial Offer, which is to continue the conversation at a later time, in my office. First I said, "the information I'm going to give you is more complex than I can give you right now," which increases the person's curiosity and desire to receive what I have to offer. But then I also offered the customized benefit of the preliminary credit check, to really seal the deal.

Making an Offer is _not_ the Same as Explaining What You Do

Talking about what you do is not the same thing as making an offer!

I was recently conducting a one-day bootcamp about Sleaze-Free Selling, and one of the women at the bootcamp experienced a huge aha moment when I covered this point. She realized that all she had been doing up until that point, was talking about what she does, without ever making an actual offer.

She would describe the different modalities she uses to heal people. Then she would also talk about why she became a healer, why she's so passionate about it, and how it is that she's trained and qualified to do the work. And maybe on a good day she would remember to throw in the results that one of her past clients got from working with her.

There's nothing exactly wrong with saying any of these things. They demonstrate that she can solve problems, and perhaps even awakens her potential customer to their own Big Problem - in other words, she's accomplishing Steps 1 and 2 of the Sleaze-Free Sales Formula. But she would stop short of the third step by not saying, "Therefore, if you want to work with me, what you should do is X, Y, X."

When this woman in my workshop finally understood that distinction, it was like a lightning bolt. She said, "Oh my God, I have to TELL people how they can get started working with me!"

Up until that point, she - like so many business owners - had been thinking that if she explained all about the wonderful stuff that she does, her customers would naturally just say, "Well great, how do I start working with you?" And of course, that's just not how customers behave! We have to lead them to water, if we want them to drink.

Now let's look at a number of case studies of clients who I helped to develop Initial Offers that elegantly led into their Big Offer.

As you're reading them, be asking yourself what small nugget of useful information can you offer that moves your potential customer in the direction of feeling like their Big Problem is being solved? That nugget is what you want to shape into your Initial Offer.

Be thinking also, of course, about how this new awakening or understanding will motivate your potential customers to take the next step with you.

Initial Offer Case Study #1: Aromatherapy Specialist

One of the people who attended a recent one-day Bootcamp I offered is Cynthia Kasper, an aromatherapy specialist in Chicago. At the bootcamp, we developed her Initial Offer.

Cynthia's business is to sell aromatherapy oils, so what she wants people to buy is $100-$200 worth of aromatherapy oil. That's her Big Offer.

But when she's at a networking event, or talking to someone at a cocktail party (which is Cynthia's primary lead generation strategy, personal networking), she doesn't have the ability to do a full work-up with someone, and then hand them a shopping bag with their 6, 8 or 10 new bottles of essential oil. Plus that would be weird to do in that setting, right?

Instead, Cynthia needed an Initial Offer that would encourage people to spend more time with her.

In her case, we decided that for her Initial Offer, she should put on a 2-hour evening workshop. This gives her plenty of time to work one on one with a small group of people, demonstrating the different oils and their benefits, and helping people decide which ones would work best for their needs. We decided the price point would be low - maybe as low as $15 - so it's very easy for somebody to say yes to attending.

You might be wondering why I didn't recommend that she offer her workshop for free. After all, isn't free easier to say yes to than $15?

Surprisingly, it's not. People often become highly skeptical about free offers. It triggers that whole "too good to be true" response. Especially when what's being offered has obvious real value - Cynthia's time, the rental of the space in which to conduct the workshop, the samples of the oils, etc.

Also, it's been my experience putting on events for many years, that the caliber of people you attract with a free event is often a lot lower than what you attract if you charge a nominal ticket price. Remember, your goal is to get people in the room who will then buy something from you. So it doesn't do you a lot of good to fill the room with people who are mostly interested in the free lunch you're offering.

The Big Problem she solves is that her potential customer has health concerns - perhaps allergies, perhaps aches and pains, perhaps sleeplessness - and they want a non-pharmaceutical solution. But they feel somewhat overwhelmed by all the options and choices in the world of natural health, so they want an expert like Cynthia to help guide their choices.

During the course of the workshop - which is her Initial Offer - she gives them answers about what kinds of oils will address their specific concerns. This makes it very easy for her to now sell them the oils, which is her Big Offer.

In the event that they don't buy any oils the evening of the workshop, she's got their name and full contact information - because they had to give it in order to register for the workshop.

This is very important when it comes time to do her followup marketing, which we're going to discuss in the next chapter.

Initial Offer Case Study #2: Motorcycle dealership

I've told you in previous chapters about my client, Marty, who owns the motorcycle dealership. The Big Problem he solves for his Ideal Customer is that the customer isn't having enough fun in his life.

So Marty's Initial Offer is that he hosts fun in-store events almost every weekend.

One of his most popular events is the Twinkie-eating contest. Now this is an event that wouldn't appeal to me, but I'm also not his Ideal Customer. His Ideal Customer is a man who's a little bit rebellious and probably trying to recapture his youth. That's the kind of man who's going to buy a motorcycle, and it's also the type of man who might love to participate in a Twinkie-eating contest.

Marty's Initial Offer is to participate in the Twinkie-eating contest. To do this, all someone has to do is come in to the store and sign up. Which - just like Cynthia's workshops - now gives him their name, phone number, address, and e-mail address. This enables him to add them to his followup marketing campaigns, after the day of the contest.

And what about his Big Offer, which is to sell a motorcycle? Marty finds that the best way to sell a man a motorcycle is to just get him into the showroom a few times, become friends with him and his sales guys, and before long the customer starts to feel just like one of the guys - and all the guys around here ride bikes!

The Twinkie-eating contest, together with all the other events he does in his showroom all year round, accomplishes this in spades. The sales guys participate in the contest too, so it's a bonding experience. Then of course after the guy has had his turn at the Twinkies, the sales guy walks him around the showroom, discussing whether he wants this bike or that one, one with these features or those.

You might be wondering about Marty's lead generation strategies - the methods he uses to get people interested in the Twinkie-eating contest in the first place.

Primarily, he uses direct mail. He's been in business for a long time, so he has a large database of customers that includes name, phone number and mailing address. So Marty sends a monthly newsletter, as well as numerous solo mailers throughout the month. He also uses the strategy of his telephone system, since a lot of customers call the showroom every day. So when they're on hold waiting to talk to somebody, a recorded message talks about all the events going on for the month - one of which, of course, is the Twinkie-eating contest.

Initial Offer Case Study #3: Tantra Instructor

My client Charu solves the Big Problem that her customer isn't having satisfying sex. But her Ideal Customer isn't concerned about _just_ sex - they're also on a spiritual path. And addressing both elements - sex and spirituality - is important for Charu to attract these customers.

Therefore her Initial Offer is a teleseminar, "How to Discover Your Authentic Sexuality Through Tantra Meditation." The title alone is juicy and intriguing for her Ideal Customers, so they tend to sign up in droves. (You can see Charu's actual optin page here: http:// sleazefreeselling.com/AuthenticSexuality)

During the call, she addresses their Big Problem - not having satisfying sex - by explaining the real cause, as she sees it, which has to do with energy blockages. She then takes them through a brief meditation designed to stir energy in their bodies, so they can begin to feel the blockages start to shift.

Then she explains that of course their blockages won't go away in a single 15-minute meditation (which is reasonable and acceptable to the people on the call); but that they CAN begin to experience real transformation during the weekend event she offers. That weekend, of course, is her Big Offer. And many people sign up for it after listening to the call.

To put people on this teleseminar, the lead generation strategies Charu uses most are online - specifically her blog and social media. She has been in business for many years, and has an avid following, so she reaches a lot of people with these strategies. (although she didn't have that following when she started; and her blog was the main technique she used to develop that following in the first place).

Because she relies heavily on online strategies, she also attracts a nationwide and even global audience. While a few of these people do end up flying in to attend her weekend events, she offers a wide range of products and services that are more convenient for non-local clients. She ends up selling a lot of these products and services as the result of her persistent followup marketing - which is the topic of our next chapter.

~~~~~~

Action Plan - What's your Initial Offer?

What's the Big Problem that you solve?

_____

_____

_____

What's the Big Offer you're ultimately trying to sell, and how much does it cost?

_____

_____

_____

What are the lead generation strategies you use the most? (Refer back to the Action Plan for the last chapter) Your Initial Offer needs to be something that can be easily delivered through those channels.

_____

_____

_____

What's something you can offer for free or low cost (relative to your Big Offer) that will address your customers' Big Problem, without completely solving it? This becomes your Initial Offer.

_____

_____

_____

Check yourself: does your Initial Offer ...

- address your customers' Big Problem?

- give you an opportunity to demonstrate how great you
  would be at solving their Big Problem, if they invested
  in your Big Offer?

- present your Big Offer, as an integral part of the Initial
  Offer itself?

Finally, is your Initial Offer easy and inexpensive for you
to deliver?

~~~~~~

When you put thought and care into crafting the perfect
2-Step Offer, you will sell an awful lot of your Big Offer as
the direct result of your Initial Offer.

Of course, not every customer will buy after taking their
first nibble. But if they're still intrigued, many of them
will end up buying a few days or even a few months later.
To maximize this opportunity, you need to stay in touch
with them! The next chapter shows you how to do this
easily, and without being the slightest bit sleazy.

... CONTINUE TO THE NEXT CHAPTER ...

Chapter 7: Never again allow even a single sale to slip through your fingers

In the last chapter we talked about how to make an enticing 2-Step Offer to your customers:

- One that promises to solve their Big Problem
- One that demonstrates they can trust you as the best person to help them - they can put their Big Problem in your hands
- One that makes it easy for a high percentage of customers to say "yes" to both your Initial Offer and your Big Offer - without you ever feeling like a sleaze-ball!

But what about the customers who don't say yes to your Big Offer right away, immediately after the Initial Offer?

While a certain number of people will become customers - they'll say yes to your Big Offer - immediately upon receiving and consuming your Initial Offer, a certain percentage will require some kind of additional followup before they're ready to say yes.

Unfortunately, too many business owners let a lot of these potential sales slip through their fingers because they give up if the customer says no the very first time they ask for the sale.

That's why followup marketing - the topic we'll be covering in this Chapter - is the heavy lifting of your marketing engine.

Sleazy vs. Non-Sleazy

We learned in Chapter 5 that lead generation means finding somebody who might want to buy your stuff. Chapter 6 then showed you how to use your Initial Offer as a way of acquiring their contact information. (The Initial Offer performs several functions; but one of them is certainly to help you get their name and email address or phone number).

Now that you have their contact information - and presuming they didn't buy directly after consuming your Initial Offer - it's time for followup.

Followup marketing can get sleazy if you treat your followup as a chance to bombard everyone on your list with sales pitches. "Send them stuff until they buy or die," is a phrase some marketers are even proud of saying.

Have you ever been on the receiving end of this? Have you ever gotten suckered into divulging your contact info, and now you can't stop the emails, junk mail and even phone calls from that marketer? If you have, you probably didn't enjoy it - and you certainly don't want to inflict the same thing on someone else.

The fact is however, that persistent marketing - to a large pool of potential customers -works. It's the most effective method for selling a lot of your products and services, and thus growing your business.

So if your goal is to sell more of your products and services, then you also need to become a more persistent marketer, and implement more persistent followup marketing.

But how do you do it without being sleazy?

Developing an effective, but non-sleazy, followup marketing campaign is really pretty simple when you keep in mind the essence of the sales process, as expressed by the Sleaze-Free Sales Formula:

1. ***Awaken*** your customers to the fact that they have a Big Problem.

2. ***Demonstrate***, with action as well as words, that you are the #1 best person to solve this Big Problem for them.

3. ***Make it simple, easy and painless*** for your customers to say "Yes" to taking the next step with you - ie, buying something!

Let's look at each one of the steps of this formula, and discuss ways that you can accomplish that step with your followup marketing. To see an excellent example of a followup email campaign that does all these steps right, please see Appendix A.

Within Appendix A, I've also included extensive commentary about how each email accomplishes the steps of the Sleaze-Free Sales Formula, and elegantly turns the conversation to a discussion of the Big Offer.

Awaken. Do your customers still believe, even after receiving your Initial Offer, that they don't have a problem? Or maybe they feel hopeless their problem could ever be solved. Perhaps they think the solution to their problem will be worse than the problem itself, so they opt to do nothing.

Your completed Action Plan from Chapter 4 will provide you with the basic messaging you need to include in your followup marketing, in order to help awaken your customer to their problem.

Demonstrate.   Depending on exactly what you do, you may have a few competitors who are also talking to your customer, offering to solve their Big Problem.   In some cases, you may have thousands of competitors.   How do you set yourself apart?

In the last chapter, Chapter 6, we discussed how to present an Initial Offer to your customers that not only makes it easy for them to say "yes" to getting to know you better, but which also demonstrates beyond the shadow of a doubt that you're the best person to solve their Big Problem for them. If you've done a good job of crafting your Initial Offer, many customers will say "yes" right away.

But if your customer doesn't say yes right away to your Big Offer, now it's the job of your followup marketing to continually demonstrate that their Big Problem _can_ be solved; and that _you_ are the best one to solve it for them!

Make it easy.   It's incredible, but true: some business owners are so afraid of "selling" to their customers that they actually make it difficult to give them money!   They do this by: not including a link to their product, not stating the price, or saying something mysterious like "I'll call you to discuss this further," without ever mentioning the product they'll be calling to discuss.

These are all big mistakes.   So you want to do the opposite.

You must assume, every time you reach out to a customer, that you've achieved your objective: You're talking to somebody who has the Big Problem you solve, they believe that you can solve it, and they're ready to buy from you! If that's all true, then the customer is going to want to know: the details of the product you have to sell, how much it costs, and what they need to do next in order to buy it.

So every email needs to include this information. Every postcard you drop in the mail needs to include it. Every voice message you leave needs to include it.

I received an email recently from someone who was not doing this correctly. This woman is a healer who concentrates on helping people lose weight. I myself have a few pounds to lose, and this woman's email piqued my interest so I wanted to find out what she was offering. But nowhere in the ema il did she offer anything for sale. So I sent an email to her, asking if she sells a product of some kind.

She replied, "Yes, but I want to send out my full sequence of informational emails before I tell you about what it is." Doh! I couldn't believe it. I wanted to buy right then! But she wouldn't let me.

This woman never got my business. You know why? Because I never read the rest of her emails! The emails that "finished" explaining to me why I needed her product, and presumably gave me the option of buying it. I had been interested and ready to buy after email #1. But when emails 2, 3, 4 and 5 arrived, I was too busy to read them. So she never got my sale.

Non-Persistent Followup Means Failure

Let's look at the typical sales process - the one business owners suffer through if they don't implement an effective, yet non-sleazy, followup marketing plan.

Somewhere, somehow, a customer stumbles across you and expresses some interest. So you send them some information, or perhaps you schedule a meeting. Or if the person just showed up, maybe you talk to them right then and there.

But they don't buy.

"That's OK," you tell yourself. "They were interested. I just need to follow up." So a day or two later, you send them an email, or leave them a voicemail. Sometimes, if they're a "hot" lead, you also put a lot of time and effort into drawing up some kind of proposal or contract for the customer to review.

And all too often, what happens next? The customer never gets back to you.

You feel dejected, and don't want to "bother" them with another followup. So their contact information - along with the proposal or contract you may have spent hours developing - sits in your piles of lukewarm leads on your desk, getting cool, colder, and eventually frozen solid. Pretty frustrating.

What's a better solution?

Systematized marketing that works like a charm

To be effective, your followup marketing must be systematized. You must have a strategically thought-out sequence of emails, phone calls, post cards, "drop-by's," sky-written messages or singing telegrams that you send out. And you send it out to Every. Single. Customer.

"But how can I possibly create a followup system that I send to everybody?" you might ask. "Each customer needs something different."

No they don't - not if you're following the Sleaze-Free Sales Formula.

Customers only require customized followup if you let them run the show, if you get bogged down in their "story." If, instead, you take control of the situation with the steps I've taught you in this book, you'll find that customers fall into line pretty quickly.

After implementing the Sleaze-Free Sales Formula, you'll discover that your customers:

1. all have the same Big Problem.
2. have all come to you to receive the benefits of the same Initial Offer.
3. all said no (unless, of course, they said yes!) to the same Big Offer, for the same handful of reasons.
4. all need pretty much the same support and education from you in order to shift to a "yes."

And how do they get this "support and education" from you? The support and education that will shift them from "no" to "yes?" From your followup marketing, of course!

When you look at your followup marketing through that lens, doesn't it seem pretty easy to send the same basic sequence to everybody?

Implementing your followup campaign

Once you know what your messages are going to say, how are you technically going to say them? There are almost as many followup strategies as their are lead generation strategies. Here's a run-down of the most common, and what kinds of messages they're best for.

Email Followup

Email Followup Strategy #1: Personal Email

In the last 20 years or so, personal email has become one of the most common communication strategies on the planet. Whether it's gmail, yahoo or your company's personal email account, you're undoubtedly familiar with it. You type in a name, add a subject line and say what you want to say.

This form of email followup, to one person at a time, is most effective when it's part of an on-going communication with a potential customer. Think of it as being interchangeable with voice mail.

Email Followup Strategy #2: Newsletters

A great way to stay in touch with your entire list of potential customers via email is with an email newsletter. Newsletters increase brand name awareness; they enhance your reputation as an industry expert; they have a longer shelf life than other forms of marketing, and they also get read by multiple readers! Plus, well-done newsletters reflect some of your personality so they're a great way to differentiate yourself from your competitors.

Another important reason that newsletters are so effective is that people read them with their guard down. They're expecting to get caught up on the latest news, not given a pitch about something. So when you do slip in a little bit of an offer, it's not rejected as a sales pitch, but rather it's considered as a possible option.

Newsletters are an extremely "soft sell" variation of followup. They work because they typically get a very high open rate - meaning, people read them more than they read your other messages.

The trick to making this strategy work is to provide consistent, useful information to your customers. Information which gently demonstrates that you are somebody who can solve their Big Problem for them.

There's a service called No-Hassle Newsletters that's offered by my friend Jim Palmer. You can find out more about this service - plus get a bunch of free newsletter advice - by clicking here: http://sleazefreeselling.com/NoHassleNewsletters

Email Followup Strategy #3: Facebook and Twitter Direct Message

Nowadays, I correspond almost as much via Facebook message as I do in my regular inbox. I personally don't use Twitter or LinkedIn nearly as much as Facebook, but they work pretty much the same way, for the same reasons.

Connecting on social media is, by definition, a more social way of staying in touch. That makes it a more acceptable form of connection for some people than opting in to your email list, or agreeing to set up a meeting for an initial consultation.

The people who I talk to on Facebook via direct message tend to be people who have heard me speak somewhere - especially if I had any conversation with them before or during the speaking engagement. They were inspired by my talk and want to stay connected to me - so they send me a friend request. I then have a process of categorizing them that my VA implements for me, that allows me (or the VA, depending on the situation), to send appropriate followup messages over time.

You can also use social media as a relationship-building tool. See the section about social media further on in this chapter.

Email Followup Strategy #4: Broadcast or Autoresponder Services

Managing your email list can be quite a task. If you have one or two people on your list, you can write emails to each person. Ho wever, as your list grows to 100's or even 1000's of subscribers, this would take too much time. You still want to reach out to your subscribers though right?

After all, every person on your list is a potential paying customer. So how do you have time to talk to all these potential customers, and still have time to run your business? An autoresponder service is the answer.

After people visit your website and leave their contact info in exchange for your Initial Offer (your Free Report, or whatever you've decided to use), now you can send them a pre-programmed sequence of messages, via your autoresponder.

The first message should be a welcome message, right after they sign up. The remaining emails should take them further along the path of the Sleaze-Free Sales Formula: awakening them to their Big Problem, demonstrating that you're the #1 best person to solve this problem, and making it easy for them to say yes to buying from you.

Your autoresponder service has a lot of flexibility. Messages can be sent daily, once a week, or on whatever schedule works for you. They can also be scheduled to be sent at a particular time of day, or on a certain date if you prefer.

You may have heard of some of the services that provide this kind of service. They include iContact, ConstantContact and aWeber. There are also more robust services that allow you to sell online products and services via a shopping cart, in addition to simply sending emails. These services include 1ShoppingCart, InfusionSoft and OfficeAuto Pilot.

I find that for most business owners, aWeber provides the best combination of robust services and a low price. To find out more, click here: http://sleazefreeselling.com/aWeber

Telephone Followup

With email's mass adoption, to say nothing of the advent of text messaging, the telephone seems like an ancient technology. While it may be an oldie, it's a goodie. More sales are closed over the telephone each year than online - by far. (excluding sales of pornography, which skews every online metric that exists)

Whether you're using the telephone to follow up with existing customers, cold leads or the newest prospects in your funnel, some basic telephone guidelines are good to keep in mind:

1. Know why you're calling. Which part of the Sleaze Free Sales Formula are you implementing on this call?

2. Get to the point quickly. When someone takes your call - especially if they're not expecting to hear from you - you have a window of less than 15 seconds to hook them or lose them.

3. Listen more than you talk. As part of your Action Plan for Chapter 4, you figured out what are the biggest reasons customers have for saying "no" to you. Then you sat down and developed some specific strategies for helping them get over their own doubts and fears, in order to get them into a "yes."

   When you're talking to someone on the phone, you should be listening for clues that indicate which version of "no" is going through their head, so that you can say exactly the right thing to shift them to a "yes."

4. Get into the right frame of mind before you call. If you're dreading the conversation, it's not likely to go well!

Postal mail

Direct mail is a marketing tactic that many business owners turned away from back when the internet became the hot new thing. Direct mail was perceived as unnecessarily expensive, when you could just put up a web page or send an email and get thousands of dollars pouring in with the click of a button.

Now that many business owners are learning that the internet isn't quite as quick and easy as they may have thought, direct mail is regaining popularity. But regardless of its popularity, it has always been the tactic that more American fortunes have been built upon than any other marketing strategy.

I discussed earlier in this book how you can use Direct Mail as a lead generation strategy. And, it's equally viable as a followup strategy. Followup is what we're going to discuss in this chapter.

However there are a number of moving parts that you must address in order to be successful with direct mail followup campaigns:

- Your list. Who are you going to mail to? If you're using Direct Mail as a followup strategy, then you'd be sending to your existing list. But you can also buy or rent lists of names from list brokers, and use Direct Mail as a lead generation strategy.

- List segmentation. Regardless of what list you use, you're well-advised to send a different marketing campaign to different segments of your list. Customers who haven't bought in over a year won't respond to the same message as a customer who bought within the last month. And if they've never bought from you at all, well then they warrant yet a third message.

- Frequency. Can you mail your list every month? What about quarterly? Are there certain direct mail campaigns that are most effective when they're done seasonally?

Once you make these decisions, the question then becomes, what exactly are you going to mail? A postcard? A letter? A newsletter? A package of some kind?

Direct Mail Variation #1: Lumpy Mail
Unlike "flat" mail, Lumpy Mail is dimensional, actually "lumpy" so it literally stands out from the typical clutter in your customer's mailbox. (Kinda like the image below "stands out" from the paragraph!)

Why does this matter?

Lumpy vs. **Flat**

Consumers have become immune and resistant to advertising. The only way to ensure people notice, open and respond to your mailing is to *get their attention in a unique way*. And if you got an envelope with a big bulge in it, wouldn't you be too curious not to at least open the thing up?

Like with everything, there are nuances to becoming successful with Lumpy Mail.

My colleague, Jon Goldman, is a business owner who has achieved off the charts success and a certain degree of notoriety as well, as the creator of Lumpy Mail. (You may have heard of his stunt of mailing a watermelon to a customer?)

He offers a free course, "The 7 Secrets to getting your mail opened and getting great response rates" that you can check out by visiting http://sleazefreeselling.com/LumpyMail

Direct Mail Variation #2: 3D Mail

The only difference between 3D Mail and Lumpy Mail is the brand - it's like Kleenex and Puffs. And the guy to talk to when it comes to 3D mail is Travis Lee.

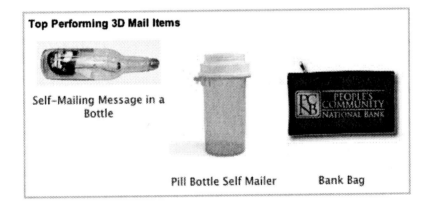

Top Performing 3D Mail Items

Self-Mailing Message in a Bottle

Pill Bottle Self Mailer   Bank Bag

Travis offers a free course too, "The Definitive Guide to Using 3D Mail in Your Marketing Campaigns." His course includes a digital swipe file that gives you free sales letters you can use for each 3D mail item.

Click http://sleazefreeselling.com/3DMail to learn more about what Travis can do to help grow your business.

Direct Mail Variation #3: Personalized URLs
Personalized URLs, or PURLs, are now an important strategy in both email and print marketing to deliver personalized content to potential customers. Implementing PURLs involves creating a specific landing page for each recipient in your campaign. The PURL itself can then be included in the postcard or letter you send out.

Amazing as this may sound, PURLs can be specific to one person, so each of your customers has a unique PURL. By utilizing the person's name, it really grabs the eye of your customer, and that's what you're driving for.

So for instance, if your website is www.SleazeFreeSelling.com, you could create PURLs like www.SleazeFreeSelling.com/JohnSmith - and then print it on a postcard or insert it in an email that you sent to John Smith.

PURLs also provide you as a company a great advantage in tracking the response of your campaign. With PURLs targeted to individuals, you'll know exactly who is accessing your web site, when they're visiting and what they end up doing at your site. This valuable information will allow you to make relevant follow ups to the people that visit, as well as to those that don't.

There are a number of companies who can help you with PURL marketing, but one that I recommend can be found at http://sleazefreeselling.com/PURLs

Text Message

Text message is a technology for follow up marketing that's on the rise. It's a brand new one that's coming in, and people are trying to figure out how to do text message marketing. It's not very common, not a lot of marketers yet do it, but it's on it's way in, as a follow up marketing strategy.

To learn about Text Message marketing, and receive a free Mobile Marketing Strategy Session, check out http://sleazefreeselling.com/TextMessaging

Text message followup is also included within the Instant Customer system, which I describe below.

Social media

If you know your potential customer is active online - they have a blog, they post a lot on Twitter or Facebook, they create frequent YouTube videos - you can make it a point to follow them in these places, and interact with them whenever they post new content.

In most cases, this is a rather indirect path to a sale. But it can be a very powerful one. After all, you don't want to comment on somebody's Facebook wall, "Interesting problem you're talking about here - I could help you with that, if you'd just sign up for coaching with me!" Of course, that would be kind of sleazy.

However, the big value of social media commenting is that it strengthens the relationship over time. It's a pretty casual way to keep your face and name top of mind

- since we all tend to look at the interaction we get on our social media stuff. Plus, who doesn't like it when someone adds to their likes and comments and retweets and shares?

So when an opportunity to talk about your Big Offer DOES present itself - either at the next live networking event, or when they receive your email newsletter, or when you call them to follow up a few weeks later - it's likely that your social media interaction with them will have softened the beachhead, so to speak.

This strategy works best when you sell a high-ticket item, and you have a rather long sales cycle with a specific Ideal Customer.

Instant Customer

One of the most comprehensive services on the market for managing all your followup marketing is Instant Customer.

Instant Customer is a software system that integrates 7 different followup strategies, including email, text message, voice message and more.

It also allows you to capture your customer's information via a wide range of methods: an optin form on a website, via text message, a QR code, business card scanner - even with voice mail. Yes, the system lets your customer's dial a local phone number, leave their information and thereby be entered into your followup marketing campaign.

The system is so robust, I couldn't do it justice here. But they've developed a free series of 21 videos that explain all the features of the service, and all the benefits of using it.

Hint: If you're an author, there's a feature of Instant Customer called the Receipt Robot that can skyrocket your book revenues.

To learn more about what Instant Customer can do for your business, sign up for their video series here: http://sleazefreeselling.com/InstantCustomer

~~~~~~~~~~~~~~~~~~~~~~~~~~~~~~~~~

Action Plan - How to develop a winning followup marketing campaign

What are the questions a potential customer might have after receiving your Initial Offer? (What questions do people tend to ask you?)

_____

_____

_____

What are the fears, doubts and insecurities that might be preventing them from buying?

_____

_____

_____

What can you tell them to help overcome those doubts
and fears? (Refer back to Chapter 4 to help you with this)

_____

_____

_____

What can you say about your own ability to solve their
problem? (testimonials are far and away the best way to
communicate this)

_____

_____

_____

In what way can you re-state your Big Offer, in case they
misunderstood it or simply weren't compelled by it, the
way you explained it in your Initial Offer?

_____

_____

_____

Conclusion and Next Steps

If you've done the work I've prescribed in this book, you have created for yourself a well-oiled machine that attracts customers in droves, who are primed and ready to say yes to your products and services.

1. You've identified a Big Problem that most (but definitely not all) of your past customers suffer from - one that you are exceptionally good at solving. This is the same Big Problem that most of your FUTURE customers are likely to be suffering from!

2. You've written a description of your Ideal Customer - the person you can help the most - and agreed in your mind to stay focused on serving only customers who fit that description.

3. You've shifted your attitude about why customers sometimes don't buy. Instead of "How can I get them to buy?" you now ask yourself, "How can I help them escape their own fear, doubt and hopelessness?"

   You've also written out a number of good answers to that question, based upon the biggest fears and doubts you encounter from your customers.

4. You've determined which two or three lead generation strategies you're currently using that are the most effective. You've also committed to learn about - and then implement - at least one, but no more than 3, new strategies to attract lots more of your Ideal Customer.

No more haphazard customer acquisition for you! You <u>know</u> where your customers come from - and if you need more of them, you're confident (or will soon become confident) that all you need to do is invest more time or money in lead generation.

5. You've developed a juicy Initial Offer - one that attracts your Ideal Customer like moths to a flame. Plus, it elegantly lays the groundwork for you to talk about - and your customers to say yes to - your Big Offer.

6. You've created a winning followup campaign - one that ensures you will never let another sale slip through your fingers. And best of all, you've put it on autopilot! So you can be out enjoying your life, while your automated followup marketing systems are busy nurturing prospects into customers for you, 24/7.

And, you've done it all without being even the tiniest bit sleazy!

That's right. When you follow the 3-Step Sleaze-Free Sales Formula I've outlined in this book, you will not only get rich selling tons of your products and services, you will also become a knight in shining armor (or Knightess?) to every single one of your customers. Because you haven't sold them something out of your need, you've simply helped them to buy it out of theirs.

You - that's right, you - have solved a Big Problem for your customer. One that nobody else before you has been able to solve. And for that, your customers are deeply, deeply grateful.

~~~~~~

Now What??

If you've enjoyed this book and want more, here are some resources for you:

Check out my blog, http://SleazeFreeSelling.com - and be sure to sign up for my newsletter while you're there.

Register for my next "Don't Be Sleazy!" one-day bootcamp by clicking here: http://sleazefreeselling.com/LiveWorkshop If you can't attend live, you can always attend remotely, via live stream.

If personal coaching is what you're after, please submit an online application on my website: http://sleazefreeselling.com/CoachingApplication

URGENT PLEA!!

Thank you for downloading my book. Please
REVIEW this book on Amazon. I need your
feedback to make the next version better.
(If Zoe can do it, you can too!)

Thank you so much!

Appendix A: Follow-up Email Sequence

The following email sequence was written by a client of mine, Alexis Neely, of Law Business Mentors. Customers of Alexis's (who, in this case, are lawyers) receive this sequence after having given their name and email address online in exchange for Alexis's Free Report, the Law Business Manifesto.

The Manifesto is her primary Initial Offer. In the Manifesto, she completes the steps of the Sleaze-Free Sales Formula, and then elegantly presents her Big Offer, which is a home study course for lawyers about how to attract more clients.

But as you'll see when you study this email sequence, this sequence itself is also an Initial Offer. Because Alexis knows a little secret: a lot of people who ask for her Manifesto won't ever read it! That's why she repeats a lot of the steps of the Sleaze-Free Sales Formula here in this email sequence.

At the top of each email, I've provided specific commentary about what Alexis is accomplishing in that email, and how you can model her for success with your own followup marketing.

Logistical items to pay attention to

In order for your followup marketing to be effective, it is critical that you keep things organized. This is true whether you have 5 team members all working on parts of your followup engine, or if it's you all by yourself behind the computer.

One important aspect of this organization is to include all the pertinent information at the top of every email. You'll notice in Alexis's emails below, there are four fields at the top of every email: the date to send on, the template title, who the email is from and the subject.

The **date** to send on can be either a calendar date, or a "days in sequence." Most often, your followup emails will be sent on a particular day in the sequence, rather than a calendar date. So the first email will be sent immediately after they opt in; the second email will be sent the following day (the first day in the sequence); the third email will be sent 3 days after that (the 4th day in the sequence), etc.

The **Template** title is a field that's particular to Alexis's shopping cart program, which happens to be InfusionSoft. If you're using a different software program, this field will either be unnecessary, or will be called something different. But it's how you locate the email within your software program, after you've written it.

The **"from"** field may seem unnecessary to you. "The email is coming from me - who else would it come from?" you may think to yourself. But what if you have more than one business? Or more than one email address you use? This field is also essential if you're having an employee of any kind send these emails for you, so they are assured to not make any mistakes.

The **subject line** is the most important element of any email - because without a good subject line, your email won't get opened. It's amazing to me how often business owners write an email (or even a whole campaign) and forget to think about the subject line!

Personalization

Have you ever received an email from a company that included your first name in the subject line, or someplace in the body of the email? Doing this is called personalization, and every autoresponder service allows you to include it in your emails.

You'll notice many of Alexis's emails below include personalization in both the subject lines and the body of the emails.

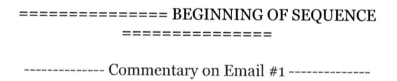

================ BEGINNING OF SEQUENCE ================

--------------- Commentary on Email #1 ---------------

In this email, Alexis awakens the customer's problem by saying things like:
- lawyers everywhere struggle to grow their practice
- the traditional law firm model has us stuck on a never-ending merry go round
- unpredictable, uneven cash flow

Then she demonstrates that she can solve the problem by saying in the PS:
- I am going to be giving you resources I paid more than $20,000 to create for my own law firm, which will help you increase the profits in your practice while reducing your workload.

Finally, she makes it easy for them to get started by telling them not once, but twice, how to access the free Manifesto they've just opted in for:

Get your copy of the "Law Business Manifesto" here in our New Law Business Model members' site:

Law Business Manifesto
User: ~Contact.Email~
Pass: ~Contact.Password~

---------- End of Commentary on Email #1 ----------

Send on: Immediately
Template Title: LBM Email Day 1: Welcome Email
Email From: Alexis Neely /
support@newlawbusinessmodel.com
Subject: [NLBM Gift] Welcome to the Law Business Revolution, ~Contact.FirstName~

Hi ~Contact.FirstName~,

You have made a great decision to join the Law Business Revolution, put in place a new law business model and transform your practice into a business that serves you, your clients and the world.

To thank you for joining us in our mission to revolutionize the old, out-dated and broken law firm business model, **we are giving you the first of what will be over $20,000 of practice-building, time-saving, money-making resources that I created and used in my own law firm** as I built it from scratch into a million dollar per year revenue generating business.

But first a question:

Remember _why you went to law school?_

For many of us, it's been some time, so we might not have thought about that for awhile.

My guess is that you **wanted to make a difference, be an advocate, impact people's lives for the better.**

When you read the Manifesto, you will see why lawyers everywhere struggle to grow their practice.

Get your copy of the "Law Business Manifesto" here in our New Law Business Model members' site:

Law Business Manifesto
User: ~Contact.Email~
Pass: ~Contact.Password~

What you'll see when you read the Manifesto is that the **traditional law firm model has us stuck** on a never-ending marketing merry go round and cash flow roller coaster -- never being able to relax.

This **cycle also sticks us with uneven, unpredictable cash flow** that would make even the hardiest soul sick to her stomach.

Finally, what you'll understand when you are done with the Manifesto is **how to solve the broken business model problem, find the support you need to act on it, and get moving to the law practice you've always dreamed is possible.**

To Your New Law Business Model,

- Alexis Neely

PS: Over the next few weeks, I am going to be giving you resources I paid more than $20,000 to create for my own law firm, which will help you increase the profits in your practice while reducing your workload.

My suggestion is for you to review these gifts as soon as they come out so you'll be ready when it's time to take action.

For now, log in to our member's site and grab the Manifesto:

Law Business Manifesto
User: ~Contact.Email~
Pass: ~Contact.Password~

======================================

-------------- Commentary on Email #2 --------------

In the introduction of this email, Alexis triggers something called "social proof" - she says "The response ... has created quite a firestorm!" In other words, she's saying, "Everybody read this - you should too."

Then she goes on to not only provide additional social proof, but she also heightens curiosity by saying, "The great majority of lawyers thought I was dead on about what I said, but a few people did not like it at all."

She awakens them to their problem by saying, "The New Law Business Model is for lawyers who are simply not satisfied with the status quo, really want to serve their clients the best they possibly can and live a great life while they are doing it."

She then demonstrates she can solve the problem by saying, "Anyway, today's gift will show how you can double, triple or quadruple your business, no matter where you live."

And of course, she makes it easy for them to take action by providing the link twice.

------------ End of Commentary on Email #2 ------------

Send on: 3 days later
Template Title: LBM Email Day 3: Fear Into Faith
Subject: [NLBM Gift] Worried about having enough business? Listen now.

Hello again ~Contact.FirstName~,

The response to the first gifts I gave you as part of the Law Business Revolution, especially the Law Business Manifesto, have created quite a firestorm!

The great majority of lawyers thought I was dead on about what I said but a few people did not like it at all.

The New Law Business Model is for lawyers who are simply not satisfied with the status quo, really want to serve their clients the best they possibly can and live a great life while they are doing it.

Anyway, today's gift will show how you can double, triple or quadruple your business, no matter where you live.

Joining me on this call were lawyers whose businesses doubled, tripled or quadrupled last year, in a bad economy, by following specific strategies, which I share on the call.

They'll tell you exactly how they did it and I'll give you the steps you can take right away to duplicate their success.

Download & Listen to the Call Here.click here
Fear into Faith
User: ~Contact.Email~
Pass: ~Contact.Password~

To Your New Law Business Model,

~ Alexis Neely

P.S. After you listen to the fear into faith call, I'd like to hear your comments. Share your comments about the call and read the comments of others inside our member's only site.

Login and listen now:

Fear into Faith
User: ~Contact.Email~
Pass: ~Contact.Password~

P.P.S If you are enjoying these resources, you might really LOVE the new free video training series we just created -- it's all about how you can take control of your schedule, make a real difference in your clients' lives and make a GREAT LIVING while you do it.

You can get the video training for free by clicking here.

===================================

--------------- Commentary on Email #3 --------------

In this email, Alexis awakens them to a slightly different problem: "what if I could take billing your time and sending invoices off your calendar while putting way more money in your bank account?"

She then demonstrates she can solve that problem by saying, "After shifting my model completely so I was never billing hourly and didn't even have to invoice my clients, I felt a huge sense of freedom and relief."

She then inserts a line in the PS that turns her Initial Offer (the free fee schedule she just gave them) into an upsell for her Big Offer: "If you'd like to learn HOW to use the fee schedule and create one just like it for your practice, check out our Client Engagement System here and start earning what you deserve by engaging more clients at higher fees."

------------ End of Commentary on Email #3 -----------

Send on: 5 days later
Template Title: LBM Email Day 5: From Hourly to Packages
Subject: [NLBM Gift] No More Hourly Billing or Sending Out Invoices w/ This Resource

Hello again ~Contact.FirstName~,

How have the manifesto and audios have been for you so far. Have you made time to read and listen or are you just too darn busy?

Well, what if I could take billing your time and sending invoices off your calendar while putting way more money in your bank account?

Would that free you up some time?

It did for me. I remember in the early days of my practice, it would often feel as if it was costing me more to bill my time than I was bringing in.

After shifting my model completely so I was never billing hourly and didn't even have to invoice my clients, I felt a huge sense of freedom and relief.

The resource I am sharing with you today cost me over $10,000 to develop and is essential.

Download the fee schedule I created in my office (and is now used in various forms and variations by hundreds of lawyers I have trained throughout the country who have been trained in the New Law Business Model way).

Get the Fee Schedule here
User: ~Contact.Email~
Pass: ~Contact.Password~

To your new law business model,

- Alexis Neely

PS -- This fee schedule took me literally two years and more than $10,000 to develop, but it paid for itself the first time I used it.

If you'd like to learn HOW to use the fee schedule and create one just like it for your practice, <u>check out our Client Engagement System here</u> and start earning what you deserve by engaging more clients at higher fees. *It's so cool when your clients start choosing to pay you more!*

==

--------------- Commentary on Email #4 ---------------

In this email, Alexis uses a list of well-written bullet points to awaken her readers to problems they might be having; and throughout the email presents the interview with this best-selling author as a solution.

------------ End of Commentary on Email #4 ------------

Send on: 7 days later
Template Title: LBM Email Day 7: A Whole New Mind
Subject: [NLBM Gift] A Whole New Mind (Yes, It's Possible!)

Boy, do we have a special treat for you ~Contact.FirstName~!

Today, as part of the complimentary gifts you're receiving from the Law Business Revolution to inspire you to a New Law Business Model, I want to give you the link to a quick, but **EXTREMELY powerful interview I did**

with New York Times best-selling author Daniel Pink.

The information contained on this MP3 will literally transform how you think about your life, career, and business...and I can't wait for you to hear it!

Get the Dan Pink Interview here

User: ~Contact.Email~
Pass: ~Contact.Password~

Dan graduated from Yale with a law degree, but never practiced law. Instead, he worked in the White House as the Chief Speech Writer under former Vice President Al Gore and in other positions in politics and government.

But most importantly for all of us, **he wrote the best selling book "A Whole New Mind" and his newest book, "Drive."**

Both of these books are DIRECTLY applicable to us as lawyers and **if you want to finally start truly LOVING what you do and how you do it and BEING the lawyer you've always hoped to be, you need to hear our interview.**

To give you a little taste, in this fast-paced, thought provoking interview, you'll learn...
- How 40 years of research into human motivation can help you be the lawyer you've always wanted to be.
- What it really means to be brave as a lawyer and a human being. (The answer will surprise you.)

- How to know if your practice area is right for you - and if it's not how to transition into something that is.

- How to tap into your creativity to bring more enjoyment, fulfillment and success to the practice of law. (Yes, you can exercise your creativity muscles - even if you don't think you have any!)

- Why discovering your "intrinsic motivation" will help you be more of who you authentically are in your life and work (and translate into more happiness, more freedom and really loving your life and your job/biz.)

- How having autonomy , mastery and purpose will help you make a true, lasing, positive impact on your clients and yourself.

Invest just 22 minutes and 19 seconds to listen to this interview that can serve as the catalyst for you becoming the lawyer you want to be or more of the lawyer you already are.

This interview will open up a <u>whole new mind</u> for you.

Alexis Neely

P.S. I would love to hear what YOU think after you listen to this interview with Daniel Pink. Email me at <u>alexis@newlawbusinessmodel.com</u>.

Or better yet,<u> tweet me at @lawbizmentors</u> and let me know. I'd love to connect with you there.

Here's your access again to the interview:

<u>Login and Listen Here</u>
User: ~Contact.Email~
Pass: ~Contact.Password~

==

--------------- Commentary on Email #5 ---------------

This email addresses the big concern that so many customers have - the concern that their problem simply can't be solved. (Review Chapter 4 for more information about this).

In the case of this email, the customer problem is, "maybe you do not think you have the resources to grow your practice." To help her readers overcome their own sense of hopelessness about this problem, she presents the story of another lawyer, just like them, who thought the same thing - and then found out it wasn't true. And then she uses the magic phrase, "And you can too."

----------- End of Commentary on Email #5 -----------

Send on: 9 days later
Template Title: LBM Email Day 9: Nicole Newman
Subject: [NLBM Gift] How to Find All the Money You Need to Grow Your Practice

Hi ~Contact.FirstName~,

Investing in the growth of your law practice is the single best investment you could make for your future.

With the right mentoring and support, your practice will grow into your biggest asset.

It will support you and your family during your lifetime and be an asset you can sell when you are ready to retire. (Not if you run your practice as most lawyers, do of course - but with a New Law Business Model in place, yes.)

But maybe you do not think you have the resources to grow your practice.

Nicole Newman thought that too until ...

Well, you'll have to **listen in to hear what she had to say about how she found all the money she needed to grow her practice.**

And you can too.

Go hear her story now here and **find all the money you need to grow your practice.**

Login and Listen Here

Username: ~Contact.Email~
Password: ~Contact.Password~

- Alexis Neely

PS -- after listening in, connect with me on Twitter and let me know what your next action step is to invest in and grow your practice. I'm at @lawbizmentors.

=================================

This email is where Alexis makes her Big Offer. She's been using this email sequence as an Initial Offer, to accomplish all the necessary steps of the Sleaze-Free Sales Formula. Now she is elegantly using this same email sequence to present her Big Offer.

It starts by awakening her readers to their biggest problem, right in the subject line: "What if you were engaging nearly every prospect who called your office?"

She then demonstrates that she can solve this problem by saying, "**Once I put in place my system (and it took years and a whole lot of trial & error to figure it out) I began to easily command higher fees than I ever had before, engaged just about every single person who called my office, and I pretty much eliminated cancellations.**"

To further hammer home the point that she can solve their problem, she offers numerous testimonials of other lawyers whose problems she has solved. She says, "I have since taught this system to hundreds of lawyers. You can read some of their experiences with our system here."

She also emphasizes how easy this system will be: "**The system includes specific direction on making the switch from hourly billing to a flat fee or recurring revenue model with all the _templates, scripts, checklists and training_ (for you and anyone who works for you) you need to not only know how to do it, but to actually get it done.**"

Send on: 12 days later
Template Title: LBM Email Day 12: Client Engagement System
Subject: [NLBM Gift] What if you were engaging nearly every prospect who called your office?

It's me again ~Contact.FirstName~,

Imagine what your life would be like if you engaged nearly every prospect who called your office ...
- You could probably **cut your time worrying about where your next new client is coming from in half.**
- Maybe you'd even be able to **bring on more support to free you up** from the work that really you don't need to be doing in your office.

Now what if you could double or even triple what you were charging and your new clients were actually happier to pay your higher fees?
- You would probably **be able to take less clients and provide a far better level of service**.
- Your **clients might even love you for it**. Ours did.

The Client Engagement System is a process I created for myself after continuous frustration with canceled appointments, prospects leaving my office staying they would think about it and engaging clients for fees that I knew were below the real valued I provided.

Once I put in place my system (and it took years and a whole lot of trial & error to figure it out) **I began to** easily command higher fees than I ever had before, engaged just about every single person who called my office, and I pretty much eliminated cancellations.

I have since taught this system to hundreds of lawyers. You can read some of their experiences with our system here.

The system includes **specific direction on making the switch from hourly billing to a flat fee or recurring revenue model with all the _templates, scripts, checklists and training_ (for you and anyone who works for you) you need to not only know how to do it, but to actually get it done.**

Here's where you can get your hands on my system. It pays for itself the very first time you use it.

Client Engagement System

To Your New Law Business Model,

- Alexis Neely

===================================

--------------- Commentary on Email #7 --------------

This email is extremely clever. It awakens her customers to a problem they don't even know they have - by saying "almost no lawyers know this secret ... despite the fact that it is the single most important value driver in EVERY law business."

Send on: 14 days later
Template Title: LBM Email Day 14: Membership Program
Subject: [NLBM Gift] The actual secret to your happiness in business.

Hi ~Contact.FirstName~,

I've got a HUGE Secret I Bet You Don't Know...

A radical concept - and I want to tell you.

Almost no lawyers know this secret, let alone are using it... despite the fact that it is **the single most important value driver in EVERY law business**.

After I tell you the secret, **I am going to give you a gift that could literally be worth hundreds of thousands of dollars to you** (no hype) ...and, equally as important, give you the freedom of only having to work two to three days a week.

Intrigued? You should be.
Go here to discover this secret and claim your gift.

Username: dawn@newlawbusinessmodel.com
Password: Bella123

To Your New Law Business Model,

~ Alexis Neely

PS: Think I'm being overly dramatic about this "secret"? You won't when you learn what it is. It is THAT powerful. It is THAT important.

Get it here

Username: ~Contact.Email~
Password: ~Contact.Password~

PPS: Did you hear about how Martha Hartney started having $10,000 days just two years out of law school? If not, you probably want to. And you can do it here:

http://www.LoveYourLawPractice.com

====================================

-------------- Commentary on Email #8 --------------

The problem awakened in this email is, "**This gift is a free tool to instantly increase your profits, the productivity and accountability of your staff (if you don't have a staff this will help increase YOUR productivity) without spending a penny more.**"

Like with some of her other emails, it doesn't overtly state the problem; rather, the problem is implied within the solution it presents. It directly states the benefit - or the transformation - the customer will receive when they take action.

----------- End of Commentary on Email #8 -----------

Send on: 16 days later
Template Title: LBM Email Day 16: Tracking and Productivity Tool
Subject: [NLBM Gift] Track It and Watch it Grow (a Business Tracking Tool For Your Law Practice)

Hi ~Contact.FirstName~,

Yep, it's me again with another free gift. Why? Because I know it'll take a lot of trust to inspire you to try out the New Law Business Model with me.

But once you do .... well, you'll be hooked on the freedom, the impact, the money, and the happiness.

I'm willing to do what it takes to build your trust because the world will benefit when you decide to implement some of what I'm sharing with you in your law practice.

This gift is a **free tool to instantly increase your profits, the productivity and accountability of your staff (if you don't have a staff this will help increase YOUR productivity) without spending a penny more.**

Sound good? It is. It's very good.

In fact, this **tool will not only save you bunches of money, it will reduce your worry and help you sleep better at night**.

This is a tool that Susan, my Client Services Director at my law practice used every single day so she never dropped the ball and made sure nothing fell through the cracks.

<ins>Go here to grab your complimentary copy.</ins>

Username: ~Contact.Email~
Password: ~Contact.Password~

To Your New Law Business Model,

- Alexis Neely

PS - If you have enjoyed the gifts I've been sending you, I'd love it if you would tell other lawyers you know about it. Simply send them here to get our Manifesto:

<ins>http://www.LawBusinessMentors.com/Manifesto</ins>

Twitter is a great way to do that.<ins> Connect with me on Twitter @lawbizmentors</ins> and let me know how you have liked what I've been sharing with you.

======================================

-------------- Commentary on Email #9 --------------

This email is all about making it easy for her customers to take action.

----------- End of Commentary on Email #9 -----------

Send on: 18 days later
Template Title: LBR Email Day 18: Client Service System
Subject: [NLBM Gift] Your Clients Will Really Love This

Hi ~Contact.FirstName~,

I've been getting a lot of questions from lawyers who aren't sure how to take the next step with us, but very much want to after sampling what we have to offer.

Some lawyers want to register for the next open enrollment period, where we'll have the opportunity for you to become a Personal Family Lawyer or Creative Business Lawyer (and get all of our programs) - NOW

Some want to join the programs - NOW.

Now, I'm not complaining about all of the requests that are flooding my inbox. Not at all! I'm thrilled that **there are hundreds of lawyers who are fired up.**

I think it's great because <u>my mission, in addition to helping lawyers build the practice of their dreams, is to change the public's perception of lawyers</u>. And the more lawyers who are using our systems, the more people will love their lawyers.

While you cannot join at this very moment, I do have one last gift for you.

It's a **full color Strategy Map** that walks you through the exact steps and procedures we take to service an estate planning client from the minute they are engaged, to putting them on our membership program, and through their entire lifetime.

Basically, I am giving you my entire client service system.

<u>Download it here</u>
User: ~Contact.Email~

191

Pass: ~Contact.Password~

Get it now and start your new law business model today,

- Alexis Neely

=====================================

--------------- Commentary on Email #10 ---------------

This last email in the sequence is one of the most powerful of all. The reason is that it directly confronts the customer's own hopelessness head on.

If the customer is reading these emails and experiencing any of the doubts, fears and hopelessness we talked about in Chapter 4, they're probably thinking, "Yeah, this stuff sounds good - but I don't think it will work for me. So I'm not gonna do anything."

This belief is SO much more common in the minds of your customer than most business owners realize.

Alexis addresses it head on when she says,

> **What if you do nothing with these practice resources and tools I've given you and everything stays exactly the same in your practice as it is now?**
>
> Would that be okay for you? Would your life just keep getting better? Can you go on as you have been or does something need to change?

Hit reply and let me know. You see, answering that single question will start you on the path to having the business you've always dreamed is possible."

And not only that - she makes it EXTREMELY easy for this Doubting Douglas to engage with the question. Because she doesn't tell him to "click here to buy." Rather she says, "Email me and tell me your answer."

She's basically offering to help them out of their own hopelessness, rather than shoving her product down their throats.

Very, very good.

------------ End of Commentary on Email #10 ------------

Send on: 18 days later
Template Title: LBR Email Day 21: Final LBM Sequence Email
Subject: [NLBM Gift] One Last Gift

Hi ~Contact.FirstName~,

We've been together three weeks now and over that time I have given you ten practice building tools that I used in my own law practice to build it from nothing into a million dollar a year revenue generating business.

I've given you these resources as gifts to use so you can get on the road to a new law business model that will transform your practice -- for the much better.

My final gift to you is a question. One I hope you will answer honestly and out loud.

What if you do nothing with these practice resources and tools I've given you and everything stays exactly the same in your practice as it is now?

Would that be okay for you? Would your life just keep getting better? Can you go on as you have been or does something need to change?

Hit reply and let me know. You see, answering that single question will start you on the path to having the business you've always dreamed is possible.

I look forward to hearing.

- Alexis Neely

The Client Engagement System Team

======================================